Journey into Mindfulness

Dr Patrizia Collard

Journey into Mindfulness

Dr Patrizia Collard

An Hachette UK Company
www.hachette.co.uk

First published in Great Britain in 2013 by Gaia Books,
a division of Octopus Publishing Group Ltd
Endeavour House, 189 Shaftesbury Avenue, London WC2H 8JY
www.octopusbooks.co.uk

ISBN 978 1 85675 329 6
A CIP catalogue record for this book is available from the British Library.

Printed and bound in Hong Kong
10 9 8 7 6 5 4 3 2 1

Publisher Liz Dean
Art direction Juliette Norsworthy
Designer Isabel de Cordova
Illustrations Abigail Read
Picture research Claire Gouldstone
Production Caroline Alberti

Any information given in this book is not intended to be taken as a replacement for medical advice. Any person with a condition requiring medical attention should consult a qualified practitioner or therapist.

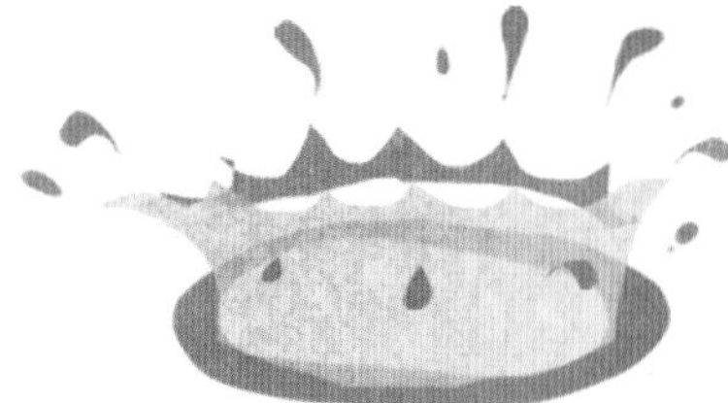

Contents

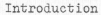

How to use this book

Our journey into mindfulness endeavours to be an aid for discovering how we can reconnect to our original way of being. Although it travels forward there is also an intention of returning back to the simple joy of being alive without needing to prove anything or achieve anything. It may be helpful to read 'The beginnings' and thereafter engage in the chapters that you are most interested in. Each chapter has a life of its own.

This book is meant as a guide to help you begin to understand and use mindfulness as an individual.

Unlike many other texts, which require prior knowledge, all you need is to approach the material in this book with an open mind.

Each chapter is designed to follow on naturally from the previous chapter, in order to provide a smooth and understandable journey. However, the chapters also stand alone in their own right, providing wisdom, knowledge and guidance without you having to refer specifically to any of the other chapters. Therefore, you can pick and choose your own pace and focus for reading.

Above all, this book is not meant to tell you what your experience with mindfulness is meant to be like. Instead, the words, the pictures, the poems and the exercises are all there for you to use and interpret as you see fit. You might like to use the poems as starting points for a meditation. Read them a couple of times and then sit with what they have evoked in you.

It is not paramount that you do all the practices within each chapter in the order in which they appear. You may choose to divide them up over a week or a month, or just leave out the practices you have no inclination to do.

I really recommend you buy a notebook to record your thoughts as you make this journey. You may want to choose one in your favourite colour or pattern, or even put stickers or postcards on or inside it, which will help you to remember your journey. The notebook does not need to include daily entries; use it spontaneously when you have an experience or insight you may not want to forget. Most of all, writing down your thoughts should be easy and fun.

Remember, there is no right or wrong way to practise mindfulness; there is only your way of exploring and engaging in it.

Chapter five

Practice: Side reach/Wind chime

Stretches the sides of the trunk and helps to keep the spine mobile.

1 Sit on a box or a chair, legs hip-width apart, feet parallel, with 90° angles at the hips and knees. Dangle your arms at your side, facing the body. Lengthen the spine and draw in the navel to the spine, engaging the pelvic floor.

2 Inhale, and when exhaling lengthen the spine, at the same time drawing the abdominals to the spine from the front, sides and the back. Keeping it slow and controlled, start to bend to your left side, holding the head in line with the spine. You will notice a light stretch on the right side of your trunk as you are moving towards the left. On your next inhalation, expand your chest and return to the start position. Repeat this movement on the other side.

3 Do this 6 times on each side.

Watch-out points

~ Make sure the head and neck stay in line with the spine.

~ Avoid leaning forwards.

~ Avoid twisting, and keep your hips facing forwards.

~ Imagine you are performing the move in between two walls; this will help you to bend without twisting.

Practice: Chest opener/Dumb waiter

Helps deepen the breathing, opens the chest, reverses hunched-forward shoulders and helps you to feel the correct alignment of the shoulders.

1 Sit on a box or a chair. With your arms by your side, bend your elbows to a 90° angle and tuck them into the waist. Keep them here and turn the palms to face upwards. The tips of the little fingers are nearly touching.

2 Squeeze your shoulder blades together. Your arms will open to the side. Feel the chest opening and then return your palms to the start position.

3 Do this 6 times.

Watch-out points

~ Keep the elbows tucked into the waist all the time.

~ Keep your spine long and supported.

~ Your head is resting lightly on the neck, like a helium balloon floating on top of the neck.

~ Keep the neck long, and relaxed, with the eyes looking straight ahead.

Chapter eight

A Daily Meditation

Let us be still for a few moments,
without moving even our little finger
so that a hush descends upon us.
There would be no place to go,
nor to come from,
for we would have arrived in this extraordinary moment;
there would be a stillness and silence,
that would fill all of our senses,
where all things would find their rest.
Everything would then be together in a deep connection,
putting an end to 'us and them', this against that;
we would not move in these brief moments,
for that would disturb this palpable presence;
there would be nothing to be said nor done,
for life would embrace us in this wondrous meeting,
and take us into its arms as a loving friend.

Christopher Titmuss

The beginnings

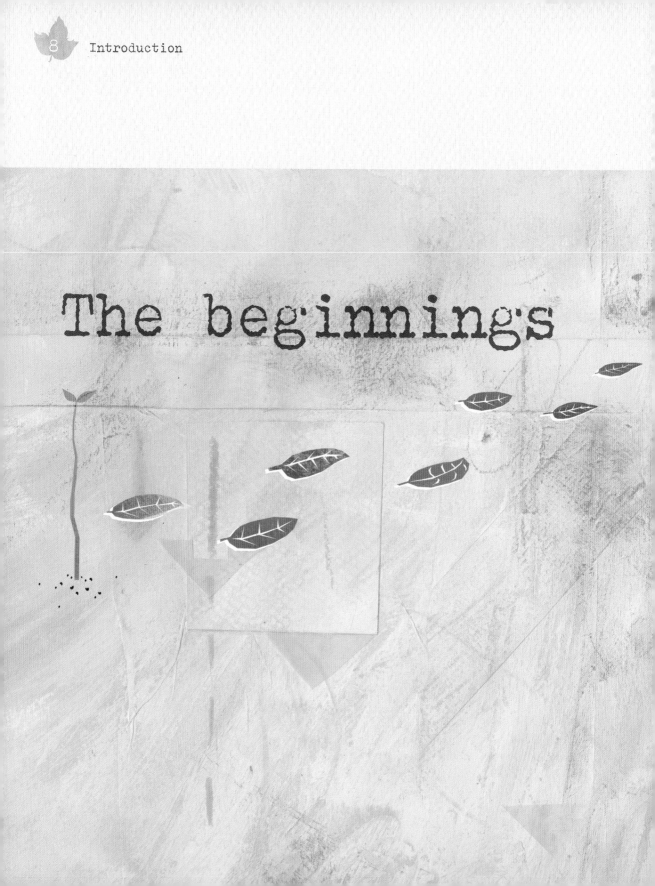

Mindfulness, as a form of therapy, has recently been in the news a great deal. It is recommended by the Department of Health and also in the guidelines set down by NICE (National Institute for Clinical Excellence), and many see it as a cheap, effective and 'doable' intervention for our stress-filled lives as much as a skill that can prevent us from actually breaking down or becoming ill.

More than 10,000 published research papers are available on mindfulness-based therapy, should you want to research the subject in depth, and there are many online videos you can watch. The application of mindfulness is used in a wide range of situations, such as parenting training, in schools, for anxiety treatment, as a relapse prevention for depression, for anger management, for the treatment of trauma, psoriasis and certain forms of cancer, and for the improvement of the immune system which has positive outcomes for patients suffering from HIV, ME (chronic fatigue syndrome), MS, eating disorders, and addictions – the list goes on and on!

Mindfulness is a new way of being, a new way of experiencing life

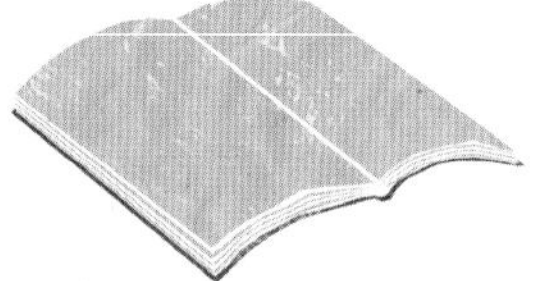

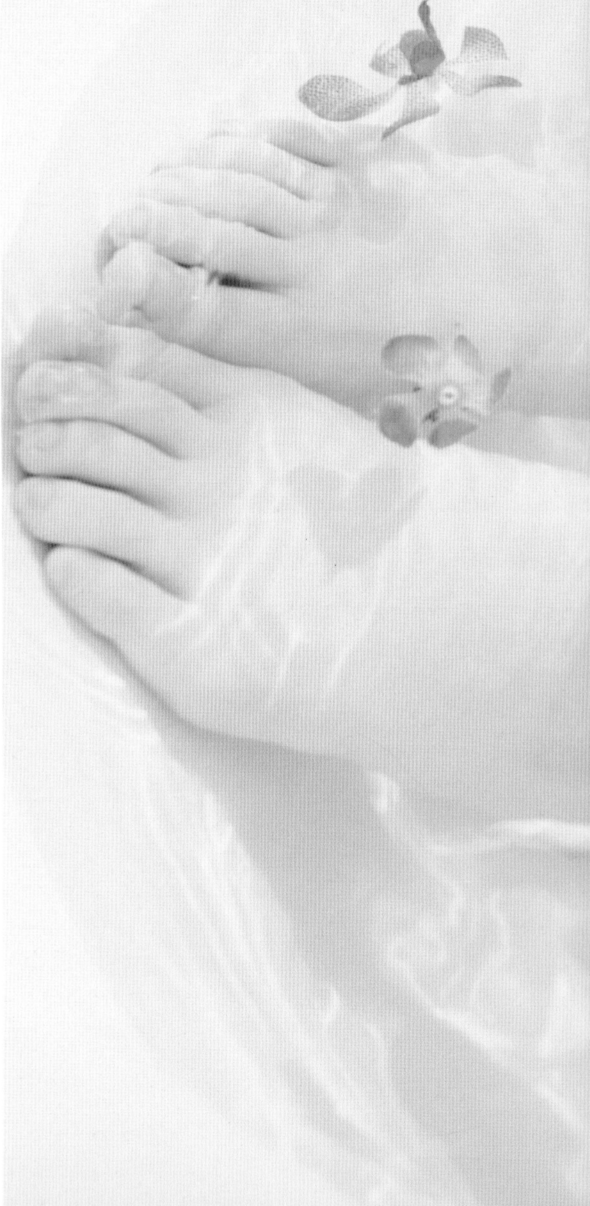

In 2008, I wrote an academic paper (Collard and Walsh) that was based on my experience of teaching mindfulness to university employees. The participants were academics, technicians and administration staff. The 'awareness training' that I taught for one lunchtime hour each week was a new set of skills to help the staff achieve a better life/work equilibrium. They were instructed to connect regularly with all their five senses and to focus non-judgementally on the here and now experience of life. The exercises I chose were neither difficult to teach nor hard to learn; I did emphasize, however, that students should ideally enter into a regular routine of practice in order for change to occur.

Mindfulness is a new way of being, a new way of experiencing life, and a way of improving one's work-life balance. The motto was: we are all different and special thus we do not attempt to become like somebody else but we may, however, be able to connect more deeply to our true self. These brief weekly sessions helped to bring about valuable changes and health improvements in the participants. Their stress levels were reduced (although Christmas was just round the corner), their language and support for each other became more compassionate and, in general, they felt more joyful and a sense of life being an adventure.

The origins of mindfulness

In the 1960s and 1970s, many people desparately wanted peace, love and enlightenment, because in the background, there was an opposing force promoting war in many parts of the world, such as Vietnam and Cambodia. There was also the Cold War which threatened the survival of the whole planet.

The origins of mindfulness are found to go back to a number of sources such as the Sutras (Buddhist writings from 2500BC), as well as other ancient wisdom traditions such as yoga, Taoism, mysticism in Christianity, and Sufism. In the 1960s, there was a 'wave of interest' that led people to travel to India and invite yogis, gurus and Buddhist monks to the USA and Europe.

To my knowledge, the first published text that really became a bestseller in Europe and the USA was a little book entitled *The Miracle of Mindfulness*, by the Vietnamese monk Thich Nhat Hanh. It was originally written as a letter while Hanh was in exile in France, to one of the brothers who had remained in Vietnam. In the 1960s, Hanh had founded the School of Youth for Social Services in Saigon. This grassroots relief organization rebuilt villages that had been bombed during the Vietnam War, set up schools, established medical centres for both sides engaged in the conflict, and resettled families left homeless and had lost everything.

Hanh's letter, therefore, was intended to support the brothers back home in Vietnam, to continue working in a spirit of love and understanding. He simply wished to remind them of the essential discipline of mindfulness, even in the midst of very difficult circumstances. When feeling overwhelmed, take refuge in mindfulness: simply being in this one moment of breath or sound, letting go of fearful thoughts. This moment, where my life is actually happening, is all that matters for now.

The Vietnamese monk Thich Nhat Hanh.

In 1973, the Vietnamese government denied Hanh the right to return to his homeland. At the time that he was writing the letter, there were several supporters from different countries who were attending the Vietnamese Buddhist Peace Delegation in Paris. So it was quite natural to think of people in other countries who might also benefit from reading this letter. Hanh suggested that the translator (an American volunteer) should translate mindfully, slowly and steadily, in order to maintain mindfulness. Thus only two pages a day were translated. Hanh encouraged the translator to be aware of the feel of the pen and paper, and also to be aware of the position of his body and of his breath, in order to maintain the essence of mindfulness while doing the task. When the translation was completed, it was typed, and a hundred copies were printed on a tiny offset machine that had been squeezed into the delegation's bathroom. Since then, the little book has travelled far.

Western awareness of mindfulness

The book has been translated into many other languages and distributed in every continent in the world. Prisoners, refugees, health care workers, psychotherapists, educators and artists are among those whose life and work have been touched by *The Miracle of Mindfulness*. Denied permission to return to Vietnam until 2005, Thich Nhat Hanh spent most of the year living in Plum Village, a community that he helped found, near Bordeaux in France. It is open to visitors from around the world who wish to spend a mindfulness retreat there, from one day to many months – all is possible. The proceeds from the sale of the fruit of hundreds of plum trees are used to assist hungry children in Vietnam. Thich Nhat Hanh has since written more than 100 books and travels frequently to spread the message of peace.

Why should we be mindful?

The 21st century is facing yet another peril, in addition to the war zones that are still scattered around the world. The new threat is something we had thought would make our life easier. Technology is changing life by the minute. We barely get used to a mobile phone or a new computer before the next, younger generation of equipment is on the market. A recent TV programme on burnout showed that more and more people use their mobile devices in bed, when having a shower and in other previously private situations. We receive emails and text messages, and unless we respond more or less immediately, people think something dreadful must have happened to us. It is a constant battle keeping up with the pace of the 21st century. Some individuals get so hooked that they can no longer find the 'switch-off' button. Driving your vehicle constantly in fourth gear, as it were, will soon end in a breakdown: whether a burnout or stress-related depression. Individuals who have gone this far may need as much as eight weeks' in-house treatment in a mental health institution to recover, and thereafter they will also need to change their lifestyle or they will just return to the 'hamster wheel' until something worse (a major physiological disease) makes them stop.

People have lost the ability to simply be, and to enjoy the moment, having just a cup of tea or eating lunch without continually working on the computer. We are all trying to multi-task and work in autopilot mode!

The result of a lifestyle that is 100 per cent different from how people lived for thousands of years is a lack of peace, lack of enjoyment and a number of destructive emotions that lead to psychosomatic disease (*psyche* means the mind, *soma* the body). Several of these perils will be discussed in the following chapters.

Connecting Eastern tradition to the West

It was just over 30 years ago that a molecular biologist, while meditating, had the inspiration to bring meditation into the secular world of a hospital. In 1979, Jon Kabat-Zinn gave up his potentially thriving career as a scientist and started a stress-reduction clinic in Massachusetts University Hospital. He had studied Korean Zen and yoga in the past and is a regular meditator.

In the early 1990s a 40-minute TV programme introduced mindfulness to a wider audience. Several thousand people wanted to learn the 'mindfulness stuff' after they watched the programme. Jon then wrote *Full Catastrophe Living* – the title is based on Alexis Zorbas in the film *Zorba the Greek*, played by Anthony Quinn, who says: 'Am I not a man? And is a man not stupid? I'm a man, so I married. Wife, children, house, everything. The full catastrophe!' Jon also developed an eight-week Mindfulness-Based Stress Reduction (MBSR) course.

A decade later, psychotherapists in Canada and the UK began to understand that mindfulness interventions may also be useful for reducing and improving psychological disorders. *Mindfulness-Based Cognitive Therapy (MBCT) for Depression* (2001) was the first publication in which the ancient wisdom was interwoven with cognitive therapy in order to help patients not to relapse into another depressive episode.

Mindfulness today

Today, MBCT and MBSR are used to treat a multitude of illnesses: anxiety, stress, burnout, chronic pain, some forms of cancer, psoriasis, eating disorders, addiction, anger, obsessive compulsive disorder (OCD), and more. When teaching mindfulness, we point out that this skill may not actually 'heal', but what it will do is change perspective on discomfort and open new possibilities for moving from just being and struggling back towards adventurous living. You learn to live around the pain rather than focus on it all the time. By reconnecting to the simple moments in life, by truly living moment by moment rather than merely existing, your focus of awareness will change. Pain in your shoulder will become a pain in the shoulder and maybe even retreat into the background of your awareness.

We have started to understand that mindfulness practice may prevent us from getting sick and unhappy, but it can also return our awareness to the childlike curiosity we all had when we were young. We may experience once again the wondrous qualities of natural life: a blade of grass, clouds in the sky, the taste of a delicious strawberry, the importance of surrounding ourselves with friends and others who care deeply for us.

We remember all of a sudden that it is these little moments that are the true wonders of being alive. These glimpses of joy really matter, because they connect us to life rather than split us from it.

The skills that we teach ourselves or try to embed into our awareness are taught not only by practising meditations regularly but also through what we call daily mindfulness. This refers to the everyday activities in which we engage and really being present during each one. A Zen saying sums it all up perfectly: 'When you drink just drink, when you walk just walk.'

Practical mindfulness

Mindfulness is being aware or bringing attention to this moment in time, with intent and without judgement. So, when we go for a mindful walk and really notice every little detail and all we encounter – trees, cars, little flowers growing out of small cracks, a lovely cat crossing the road – rather than creating to-do lists, we may at least sometimes feel once again truly enchanted with life. When we shower, we are really having a shower: we feel the temperature of the water, smell the soap, notice the muscles relaxing and feel the wetness of our skin. When we eat an orange, segment by segment, we really taste the juicy, zesty flavour, smell the citrus-like aroma and notice the texture changing in our mouth.

With all this growing of awareness, we subconsciously also increase gratitude and compassion, as can be proven by looking at Functional Magnetic Resonance Imaging (FMRI) studies of the brain. Appreciation occurs when we begin to realize what we have been gifted with, and loving kindness reconnects us to others in a win-win attitude. We start to focus on positive thoughts and perceptions, so they become less like 'Teflon' and, for a while, we let go of our fearful, anxious brain pattern, which thus may become less sticky, less 'Velcro'-like (the descriptions of 'Teflon' and 'Velcro' come from *Buddha's Brain* by Rick Hanson). In fact, every action we engage in can become a daily meditation, a slowing-down and an appreciation of life. You may wonder why you need to relearn how to be mindful – it seems so simple, in some ways, that it is almost embarrassing to have to study it.

We need only remember when we were little children. Maybe you, like me, often used to lie down in the garden (my grandmother's) and play with grass, smelt the flowers and stared at the clouds and their amazing formations. I think I was totally mindful in those blissful moments. Nothing else mattered, there was nothing to do, nothing to achieve, nothing to gain. Just simply being alive! There was no notion of time and no guilt for 'wasting' it. Time and guilt are concepts we learn about much later in life. My mother tells me that I refused to learn how to read the clock until I was seven. The little rebel in me did not want to be dominated by a square box with numbers on that was supposed to know when I was hungry or wanted to stop playing.

With this *Journey into Mindfulness* I would like to invite you to join me and remember what it is like to be consciously alive and to connect to the sense that every moment of life is precious. I would like to remind you how meaningful it can be to taste a strawberry or to smell lavender or to stroke somebody we love and really feel and connect with them.

Of course, as life is a dualistic experience, we will also become more sensitive to the painful aspects of our lives. Yet this can be advantageous too. It may prevent us from eating an out-of-date sandwich, or staying with a partner or job that is destructive to us. If we all managed to stop doing so much, even for just a few minutes a day, we would enrich our experience of life and help our bodies and minds stay healthy and well.

Each chapter in the book will focus on practices that in themselves are valuable and can be applied without needing to read the previous chapters. My hope and endeavour is to help you move closer to the stillness and joy within.

Benefits of practising mindfulness

In a nutshell, people who regularly implement some of the taught strategies may find lasting physical and psychological benefits, such as:

- Increased experience of calm and relaxation
- Higher levels of energy and enthusiasm for living
- Increased self-confidence and self-acceptance
- Less danger of experiencing stress, depression, anxiety, chronic pain, addiction or low immune efficiency
- More self-compassion and compassion for others and our planet

The Boat

To what shore would you cross, O my heart?
There is no traveller before you, there is no road:
Where is the movement, where is the rest, on that shore?
There is no water; no boat, no boatman, is there;
There is not so much as a rope to tow the boat, nor a
man to draw it. No earth, no sky, no time, no thing, is
there: no shore, no ford! There, there is neither body
nor mind: and where is the place that shall still the thirst
of the soul? You shall find naught in that emptiness.
Be strong, and enter into your own body: for there your
foothold is firm. Consider it well, O my heart!
Go not elsewhere,
Kabir says: 'Put all imaginations away, and stand fast in
that which you are.'

KABIR (15TH-CENTURY INDIAN POET)

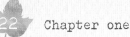

Stepping out of autopilot into the now

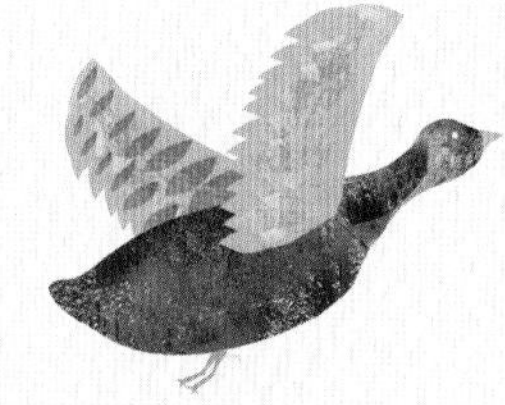

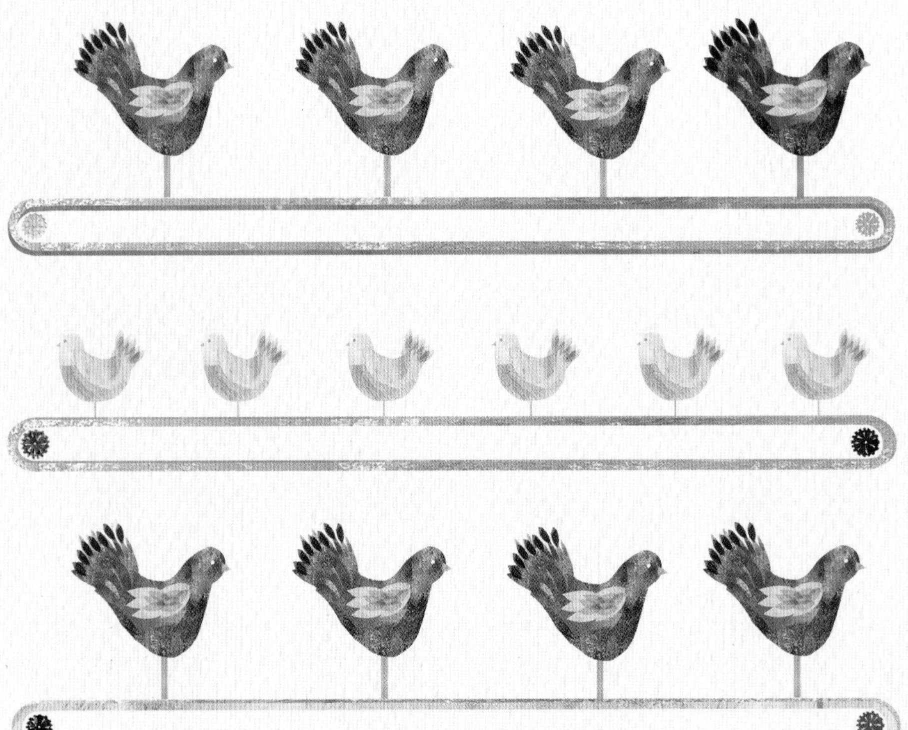

Autopilot tends to help us achieve many tasks in a day. We can sometimes even work on several projects at once, although the psychologist Ellen Langer claims that we never truly multi-task. Instead, we switch, which is actually more time-consuming, resulting in reduced accuracy than completing each task before starting the next one.

Everybody at any moment of being alive can choose to turn to mindfulness, really connecting to what is here and now. For some, this is reason enough to want to stay alive: the adventure of the moment, the ongoing newness of life, the curiosity that step by step reveals exceptional visions and experiences.

On our journey in this book, we will soon engage in a mindfulness practice where we will connect to sound. Here we link up with an experience that goes back far in our developmental stage as a human being. All healthy humans have five developed senses, which reside in the right hemisphere of the brain.

Our sense of hearing develops earlier than our sense of seeing, and listening is perhaps the first, or the most intensely developed, sense and already functional a good 30 days prior to birth. There is research evidence that 30 days before delivery, a human foetus will respond to a sudden, loud noise, and the mother will be aware of this response. I remember that my first child became particularly active when I was singing in a concert, about a month prior to his birth, and the very loud brass section started playing. I was standing in the front row, and I know for a fact that others in the audience noticed it, too.

Most of us have experienced a sense of peace when listening to calming music, to the sound of water, rain, birds and other wildlife, or being read to by a beloved voice. A great deal of our daily brain activity is left-brain activation: thinking, planning, evaluating, and so on. It is surprising we are not lopsided, considering how much we 'think and therefore feel we are' (Descartes, French philosopher) and how little time we spend truly connected to one of our feeling senses in the right brain.

All this thinking activity has one main purpose and that is for our species to survive. Mother Nature made sure that we remembered all possible dangers we ever encountered or hypothetically might encounter, and this ability helped us to survive as a species. We are rather weak, as our construction lacks strength: we have no big claws or sharp teeth, we walk on two legs rather slowly, and we do not have a particularly protective layer of skin, fur or shell. Mother Nature seemingly did not spend much time worrying about whether we feel peaceful and calm, in fact whether we enjoy life. Survival was the goal, and that job worked out rather well, considering how many other weak species are extinct now. It worked well because we have the brain with the highest cognitive functioning among the mammals on this earth.

A meeting of minds

Here is a recollection of my experience of mindfulness at Shaolin:

I enter Shaolin – the name means something like 'monastery in the young woodland' – which was built around 495AD. I am in my third year of living in China, and I have come to Henan to visit this mystical place. I am expecting a lot of action. In my mind, there will be men either in combat with each other or hitting steel posts and breaking them in two with a single, mindful hand movement. What I notice first is an incredible silence, but not a fear-evoking one. What I feel next is a sense of peace and having arrived. Then I see them – hundreds of monks, aged 5–95, in yellow robes, all sitting on the ground, eyes closed, meditating.

I ask my guide why they are doing this rather than martial arts. He explains that anybody who joins must first learn to tame the tiger within. For two years, they do nothing but sit, breathe and bring awareness to their wandering minds.

When they learn to use their bodies, they know that they are potential killing machines. So, first of all, if an enemy approaches, try to disarm them with your mind. Only as a last resort should you use your body.

Learning to switch off

There is a sacrifice we have to make on a daily basis as a result of having a highly developed cortex and amygdala (the memory and control centres of our brain), and this sacrifice causes emotional suffering. We are unable to switch off all the worrying, anxiety and horrendous ruminating thoughts that are focused on dangers that may possibly lurk 'out there'. This perpetual ability to feel fear causes our nervous system to become highly agitated and distressed.

As evolution does not happen very quickly (it takes billions of years), we need to do something now, in order to find peace and learn to be with whatever is, knowing that all states of being change again and again, good or bad, and that 'this too will pass'.

The practice of mindfulness helps us to enter a state of acceptance, where we are able to give ourselves a break from distress and enter periods of calm so we can simply enjoy being alive. Living moment by moment, seeing and feeling everything afresh, without judgement and worry, lets us experience life rather than simply getting through it.

Practice: Sound meditation

The goal of any mindfulness practice is simply to experience life as it unfolds. In order to stay present and calm and not slip back into thinking/worrying mode, we choose an anchor of awareness – a point of focus we direct our mind to. With this practice, you will connect to sound, so that you can truly experience the moment, and a whole lot of other moments, with childlike curiosity and without judgement. Entering this state of 'being' rather than 'doing' can release us from the 'worry mind' and help us 'taste' each moment as it arises. Start with five minutes and extend to longer sittings if that feels right for you. Find a special spot in a quiet part of your home or garden.

1 To start with, take a seat and sit with dignity, neither upright and rigid like a soldier, nor slumping over like a bored person. Sitting in this way will help you to be focused and aware of any sound, near and far, as it arises and passes by. Connect your mind to sound as an anchor of awareness, to prevent it from roaming freely and ending up in some anxious story once again. I recommend an upright chair that will support your spine, but is nevertheless comfortable. It helps to wear loose-fitting clothes and perhaps use a shawl or blanket to avoid feeling cold – often, when we meditate, we become more relaxed and our body temperature tends to drop a little, just as it does when we get ready for sleep.

2 Now gently close your eyes or keep them in soft focus (half-closed). Allow sounds to enter your awareness and to let them pass through it, as if they were clouds passing by in the sky. It is quite important to let go of the tendency to judge sounds as 'pleasant' or 'unpleasant'. Just allow them to be what they are: sounds from near and far, coming and going. I also recommend you let go of labelling sounds as what they stand for – a car, a bird, and so on – because as soon as we label, we tend to get involved in stories, which again trigger our left (thinking) brain, rather than our right (feeling) brain. All you need to do is to be present to sound. Listen, let it enter and pass by, sound by sound, and even listen to the spaces between the sounds.

3 You may notice that your hearing becomes more focused and that other brain activities seem to move into the background of your awareness. At other times, you may notice thoughts arising. This is the nature of the mind; it tends to get busy, even when we don't want it to. So whenever you notice the wandering mind, gently and without judgement return your awareness, your mindfulness, to simply listening. This action is your anchor!

4 You may notice after a few minutes that time seems not to matter any longer; your breathing may get longer and deeper, too. But even if 'nothing' happens and you think you are just sitting here, that is okay. Each practice will unfold differently and each person is unique. There is no right or wrong way of practising mindfulness.

Everyday practices to step out of autopilot

Whatever you do as a daily practice can become your bell of mindfulness. You may choose to brush your teeth mindfully, get dressed mindfully, listen and talk mindfully, eat and drink mindfully, drive mindfully. Many times I have heard people say: 'But I'll never get through all my chores if I slow down so much.' Maybe this is true. Maybe, however, by becoming more mindful, you may find new joy in everyday activities and eventually you may even be able to 'run' mindfully, that is flow with focus through life.

Case study

One of my clients, who suffers from very bad eczema, has to put cream all over her body twice a day. She hates doing this, but if she doesn't, she is in more pain. I was tempted to suggest to her to choose this as her everyday mindful activity. Thank goodness I didn't, mainly because she needed to find that entry point herself. As if she had read my mind, she soon did exactly what I had intended to recommend to her and something miraculous happened. Not only did she find she actually enjoyed the process of putting cream on her body more, but she experienced enormous gratitude for being privileged to have this medication. She also noticed her eczema diminishing.

Had her immune response improved? That is highly possible, but she might just have done the application with more care and precision. Anyhow, her improvement means she suffers less pain and discomfort which is really noticeable, even to others.

Moments

Less than a second
The universe was born
The stars we see so clearly
Seem only a little far
Almost touchable
But not quite
A seed breaks open
A new life
Moments
Here now
But briefly

PATRIZIA COLLARD

Being with fear

Fear and anxiety are our natural states of being, assisting us in our survival. Even though we are less often victims of physical attacks 'by wild beasts' as our forefathers, our body has only two modes of existing: the fight or flight response (sympathetic and parasympathetic nervous system). Our whole organism cannot accurately differentiate between real fears and imagined ones.

If you watch a horror film, you will have similar physiological responses as if the situation were actually happening in front of your eyes. In his excellent book *Why Zebras Don't Get Ulcers*, Robert M. Sapolsky points out how wonderful a biological system is where one only feels fear when actually needing it. For example, once a lion starts to eat the zebra he has just caught, the other zebras in the group simply start grazing again, apparently having forgotten that they had just been in real danger themselves and could have been eaten instead.

Humans, however, are quite different from zebras. We have an evolved brain, one that can remember, hypothesize and think about the future. So, for example, a healthy fear of spiders (arachnophobia) experienced by our ancestors who lived in caves or jungles no longer has real value in most parts of the world today. However, many people now do experience seeing a spider as highly anxiety-provoking. In 'fear response', they are no longer able to access their logical mind, which would point out that this little animal is a natural enemy of mosquitoes, for example, which can actually bother us much more directly at times than spiders.

Humans developed this sophisticated brain starting with the first humanoid, *Homo erectus*, approximately 1.5 million years ago, which evolved into *Homo heidelbergensis* and, eventually, into *Homo sapiens*, some 700,000 years ago. We can observe from the size of discovered skulls that human brains were constantly increasing in size, becoming more and more effective in inventing skills to survive. As our bodies are rather vulnerable – we do not have scales, long teeth or hard claws to protect us – we developed other possibilities (weapons, traps, and so on) to prevent our enemies from harming us. We do, though, pay a high price for possessing such alert brains. In *Hamlet*, Shakespeare, puts it very succinctly: 'There is nothing either good or bad, but thinking makes it so.' Our wild capacity of imagination can make life hell, unless we learn to let go of unwarranted anxiety. We are word perfect in recalling negative thoughts – as if they were superglued into our memory banks – but, alas, we are equally good at letting positive thoughts slip away – as if they were stored on a greasy pole.

Fear not only causes a lot of physical and mental discomfort, but if it is not controlled, it can lead to medical conditions such as anxiety disorders, phobias and obsessive compulsive disorder (OCD). We can nevertheless proactively and mindfully attempt to push through or be with fear, which may initially seem easier said than done. However, just as I mentioned earlier, spiders rarely cause death to humans of the 21st century, and other fears may also just be a concoction of our creative, worrying brains.

This journey into mindfulness may be one that can help you attempt gentle steps in this direction: actually being with fear, feeling it in your body and, with practice and trust, step by step learning to unlock the prison cage of fear. Just because something is a frightening hypothesis, it may in fact be quite bearable, harmless or even enjoyable. A former client of mine, who suffered from a fear of flying, is now working as a flight attendant.

Mindfulness practice, if regularly observed, can not only change the biochemistry of our body, but also change the brain structurally. The title of 'happiest man on Earth' – although he doesn't like being called this at all – has been given to Matthieu Ricard, a Buddhist monk with a PhD in molecular genetics. He has a much smaller control centre (amygdala) than other humans and can endure being in an FMRI scanner for a couple of hours. Once, when he came out of a scanner, having gone through three long meditations while being observed, he is supposed to have said that it was almost like a nice retreat. His shrunken amygdala also helps him not to blink when there is a loud noise close by. He is 'Mr Calm', but he does still mindfully check a road before crossing it.

Once again, it is most helpful when in 'anxious mode' to try to connect deeply to your physical experience in the body and, at the same time, link this connection to nature, a sound or your breathing, for example.

The Rainbow

And the heavens shed tears of silver
the golden thunder sang a wondrous lullaby
the woods kept calling spirit-elves,
beguiling man to enter here:
smell, touch, feel the softest molten ground
cascades of white wet smoke drifting upwards
filling spaces between evergreens and birches
and mingling slowly, passionately
with clouds laden with water pearls.
And beyond the canvas of the sky
the sun sent forwards gently-beaming strokes,
and it appeared – without an introduction, just so –
a bridge across sparkling lofty hues,
yellow, orange, purple, pink and blue.

PATRIZIA COLLARD

Practice: Mindful walking

Experience the miracle of moving, of being alive, of not needing to get anywhere, of letting go of fear, trusting in a practice that has a tradition more than 2,500 years old. Walking meditation can be done inside or outside, wherever it is safe and protected, so you cannot trip over. A private garden, no matter how small, is ideal. It's enough to be able to walk ten steps or so in one direction.

When we decide to walk mindfully, we first take a stance to feel really connected to the earth, feet hip-width apart and solidly rooted to the ground. First, take in the area you are to walk in, keeping your eyes open and looking straight ahead. Then, very slowly start to lift your right foot from the ground. Notice the heel peeling off the ground, and the weight shifting onto the left leg and foot. Having peeled the right heel off, observe how you are moving it forwards ever so slowly and gently placing it down exactly one step ahead. While you are placing the right foot down, you are observing the left heel beginning to peel off the ground and the weight shifting back onto the right leg.

At first, you may notice walking in a slightly wobbly way, as you have slowed down the pace so much. It may be helpful to imagine making real footprints in the ground, like walking on a sandy beach. Your awareness will be fully occupied with the lifting, shifting and placing of each foot step by step, as well as mindfully observing how your weight shifts from left to right and back again. When you have done approximately ten steps in one direction, take your time in turning around. Notice how your hips swirl around very gradually and, before starting your next set of steps, stand once again mindfully rooted to the ground.

With each passage you walk, it is possible to feel more and more grounded and safe, although each person's experience differs. Try to do it with an attitude of openness and curiosity, as would a child. Practise mindful walking maybe for ten minutes initially, then expand it gradually to 20 minutes, should you wish or need to.

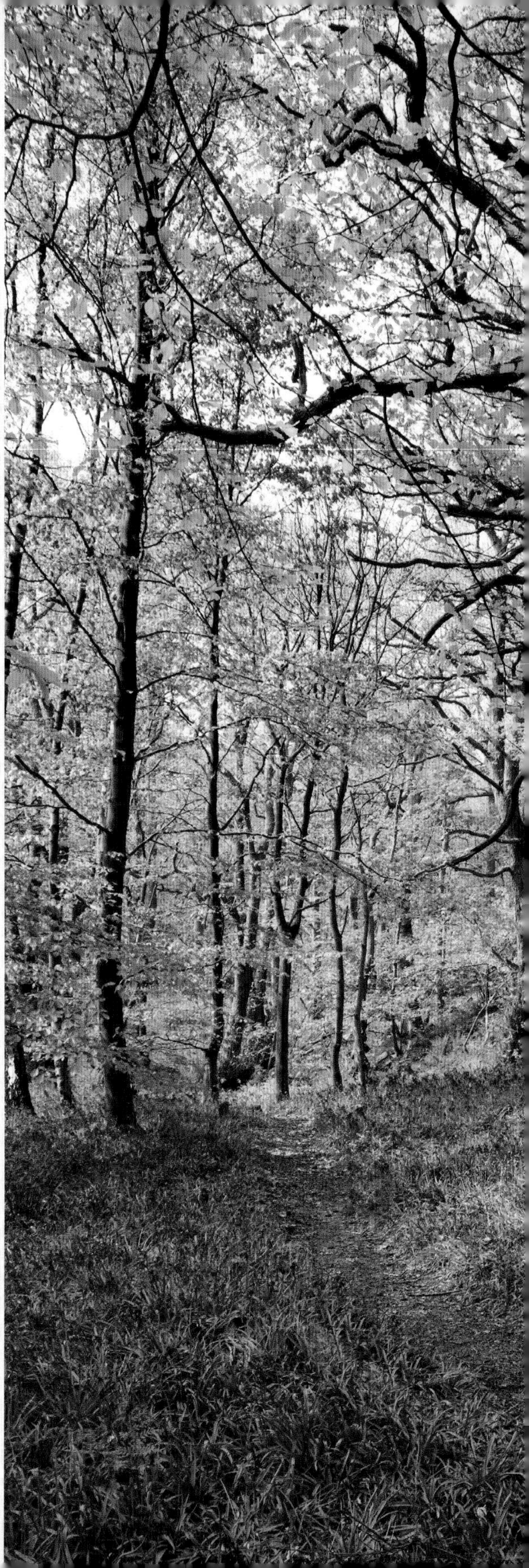

Case study

Tom frequently experiences fear. He feels he is no longer attractive and lovable – he has not been in a relationship for several years. His job is insecure and, should he lose this one, he believes he won't get another. His father has dementia and should be taken into care because he needs constant supervision. When Tom's anxiety spirals out of control, he often becomes very fidgety and finds sitting meditations difficult, so he starts off by walking mindfully until he feels ready to sit and focus on his breath, for example.

In order to stay with his walking as a focus of awareness, he likes to walk in the office. He can just about fit in ten steps. At one end of the office there is a beautiful window looking out onto a luscious green bush; at the other end hangs a poster of his favourite city. So, should his mind wander off during the ten steps he is mindfully walking, these two images are reminders to bring him back to it. Each lane he breaks down by mentally repeating 'lifting, shifting, placing'. He lifts the heel, shifts the foot forwards and then places it down. The focus on the soles of his feet and the repetitive instruction help him to centre and let go of all the fear-inducing aspects of his life. After doing this for about ten minutes, he adds a sitting practice. This combination really works for him.

Practice: Mountain pose: standing position

Strengthens your legs, improves the posture and may help you feel like a strong mountain.

1 Stand with the feet hip-width* apart, with your arms by your side, palms facing in, gently touching the thighs.

2 Take a few breaths to help you become aware of your breathing. When you are exhaling, contract the pelvic floor muscles and lift them up until you feel a squeeze at the base of your buttocks, a physical sensation as if your sitting bones are coming closer. This action supports the spine from below. Continue to breathe evenly. With the next exhalation, draw the entire abdominals to the spine and, at the same time, lengthen the spine upwards. Stand tall, with the spine straight and the head lifted. Breathe deeply and widely into the lungs, creating with each in-breath a sense of space in the entire chest area. With the exhalation, roll the shoulders up, back and down, releasing any tension that might be in the upper back.

3 Stand here and, with each in-breath, feel the uplifting in the entire spine, and with each out-breath, as you gently draw the navel to the spine, feel the support you are giving your lower back.

*The hip sockets are set in from the hip bones by 4–6 cm, so 'hip-width apart' means that the feet are within the frame of the pelvis.

Practice: Mountain pose: With arms up

Helps you control and steady your breathing and to create a sense of solidity and groundedness.

1 Stand in Mountain pose (see above).

2 Exhale, stretching your arms down, then, with the inhalation, lift your arms to the side slowly and continuously up to the ceiling until the palms face each other – the arms are either in a V-shape or slightly closer, shoulder-width apart or by the ears with the palms touching each other. Repeat, and, with every exhalation, roll the shoulders back and down; with every inhalation, try to stretch the arms a little more. If that is not possible, hold the position for 3–5 deep breaths. Return to lengthening the spine, turning the palms outwards so that their backs are touching each other. With the exhalation, start to move the arms over the side, back and down. Move slowly until you are back in the start position.

3 You may feel inspired to visualize a beautiful imposing mountain, one you have seen in real life, in a photograph or in a film, or one you have just created in your imagination. Stand with a strong stance for a few mindful breaths, seeing and maybe even becoming the mountain!

Control and steady your breathing and create a sense of solidarity

Practice: Awakening breath

Helps us to breathe more fully, and strengthens and awakens us to face the day with confidence and calm.

1 Stand in Mountain pose (see page 44), with the spine lengthened upwards and the legs and feet hip-width apart. Position the arms by your side, palms to the front, so the thumbs face outwards. This can also be practised sitting on a chair or on the floor.

2 Inhale and sweep/lift your arms slowly up and overhead until the hands meet above the head, palms touching. Exhale slowly as you lower the arms back down to your sides, moving slowly with your breathing. See if you can deepen and lengthen your breathing, and try to feel the pause after each breath.

3 Repeat 5–8 times.

Watch-out points

- Anchor your feet with the heels and the big toe and the little toe, so that you are firmly grounded.
- You can bend the elbows a little to avoid tension in the upper back.

Practice: Standing stretch/starfish

This pose strengthens the legs, back, shoulders and arms, and gives you a feeling of being centred, with energy and confidence radiating from the navel region and spine into your arms and fingertips.

1 Stand in mountain pose (see page 44), with your arms at your sides facing/touching the outer 'seams' of the thighs, fingers pointing down.

2 Step your feet apart by moving the front parts of the feet, then the heels (toe-heel movement) until they are about 50cm apart and the feet are standing parallel. Contract the pelvic floor in and up, and lengthen the spine upwards. Breathe and hold the position until you feel stable. Inhaling, lift your arms over the side up to shoulder height (you are forming a T-shape), with palms now facing down and parallel to the floor. Keep lengthening your spine upwards out of your pelvis and squeezing the sitting bones together (pelvic floor lift) to pull the tailbone down. Consciously relax the shoulders as you extend your arms and your fingertips to the sides.

3 Hold for 3–5 breaths.

Watch-out points

- Remember, your feet should be slightly turned out but keeping the heels together. and the palms are facing up.
- Keep the abdominals drawn in and the back elongated.
- Check that your knees are in alignment with your feet to protect your knees.
- Try to press the knees open as you squat and squeeze your buttocks.

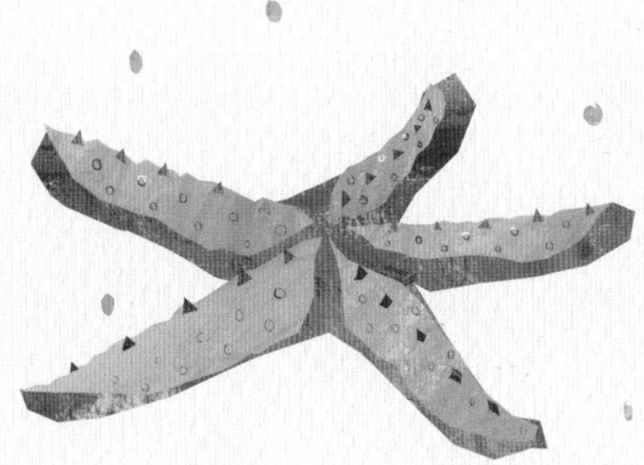

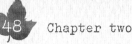

Practice: Powerful goddess/Emperor

Firms the legs and thighs, improves balance, brings awareness to the physical relationship between the pelvis and the upper body. It is also fun and a good tension-releaser and confidence-builder.

1 Stand in Mountain pose (see page 44), but with the feet/toes turned out, pointing towards the corners of the mat. Keep the knees in line with the toes, and lift the arms to the side, keeping them straight and with the palms facing up. Relax your shoulders back and down.

2 Exhale, squat down, bend your knees, making sure that they are directly over the feet. As you bend the legs, keep the spine straight, as if you are moving it between two magnets pulling the two ends of the spine further apart. At the same time and still exhaling, bend your elbows at a 90°-angle, spreading your fingers wide, palms now facing the front, and exhaling with the sound 'ha' – try it loudly. Inhale and return to the start position.

3 Do this 5–8 times, trying to squat a little deeper each time.

Watch-out points

~ Be aware not to put unnecessary pressure on knees.

~ If parallel arms are difficult, ease off and try the V-shape for the arms.

~ Avoid straining your voice when saying 'ha'.

Practice: Warrior

Strengthens the feet, legs and hips, and improves balance. Also works your shoulders and back. The lifting of the arms overhead can give you a feeling of joy like a victorious athlete or football player throwing his/her arms up to celebrate a win.

1 Stand in Mountain pose (see page 44), at the front of your mat, arms at your sides.

2 Exhale, step back with your right foot and bend your left leg at the knee, coming into a high lunge position. Your feet and hips are pointing forwards, and your back leg is straight, with the heel grounded on the floor. Firmly ground yourself into the back foot, but avoid collapsing into the inner arch of the foot. The left knee is bent above the left ankle. Take a few breaths to find your balance. Inhale and raise both arms slowly forward and up until they are close to your ears, parallel to each other, palms facing. Hold for 3–5 breaths. Look ahead and keep the shoulders relaxed; avoid hunching them. To get out of the pose, reverse the sequence as you lower the arms and step forwards with the right foot parallel to the left. Repeat the movement on the other side.

Watch-out points

~ Only lift your arms when you have found your balance.

~ Keep the bodyweight in your back leg.

~ If parallel arms are difficult, ease off and try the V-shape.

Practice: Standing side bend

Gently stretches the sides of the body, opens the ribcage to deepen the breathing, works the waist muscles, improves balance and gives a feeling of being empowered.

1 Stand in Mountain pose (see page 44). Place the palms of the hands flat against the legs at the sides.

2 Squeeze the buttocks, drawing the abdominals in and lengthening the entire spine from the tailbone to the top of the head. Exhale and slowly bend to the right side, sliding the right palm down on the thigh towards the right knee. Slide the left hand up towards the left hip as it follows the movement of the spine. Keep the head in line with the spine, looking forwards.

3 Hold for three deep breaths. Exhale and then inhale, expanding your lungs and chest, and slowly straighten your spine upwards again. Now slide the left palm down and the right palm up. The head is the last to come up. Relax the neck as you move the chin to the chest, the spine staying straight. Repeat this movement on the other side.

4 Repeat twice on each side.

Watch-out points

~ Avoid rotating the spine as you are bending; it helps if you imagine you are performing the move between two walls.

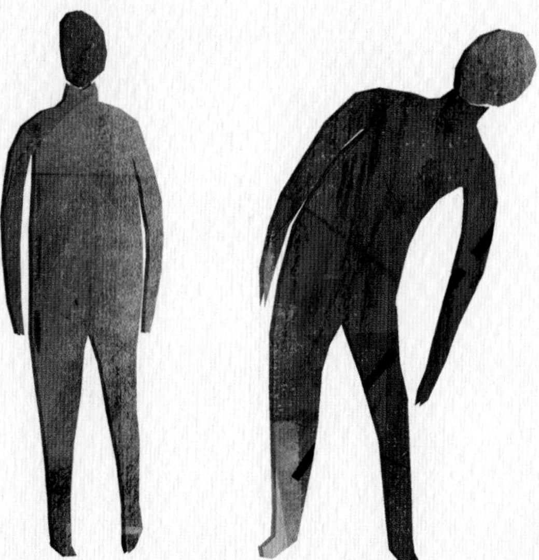

Practice: Rolling down

Increases the mobility of the spine, stretches the back muscles, works the abdominals, and stretches the hamstrings. Feel peace at last!

1 Stand in Mountain pose (see page 44), with your arms by your side.

2 Lengthen your spine, and while you are breathing slowly and deeply, bring the chin to the chest and roll forwards and down as if you are rolling over a big ball. Your hands glide down on your thighs and help you to control the movement. Slowly the body will be moving forwards and down. (With practise, you will be hanging forwards and down from your hips, and your fingertips will touch the floor in front of you, the buttocks in line with the heels.)

3 Hold the position for several deep breaths and then slowly return. Exhale to squeeze the sitting bones together, draw the abdominals to the spine, and then breathe in and out softly and deeply, straightening your spine as you roll up again, letting your head dangle, arms touching the legs to support the movement. Bring your head up last, rolling the shoulders back and down. Stand tall and be in control.

4 To modify the practice, use your alternate knee and bring it into the chest – lie on your back, feet on the floor hip-width apart. With each out-breath, relax the lower back into the ground.

5 Bring one leg into the chest, and hold and hug it to the chest. Lower the leg and repeat with the other leg.

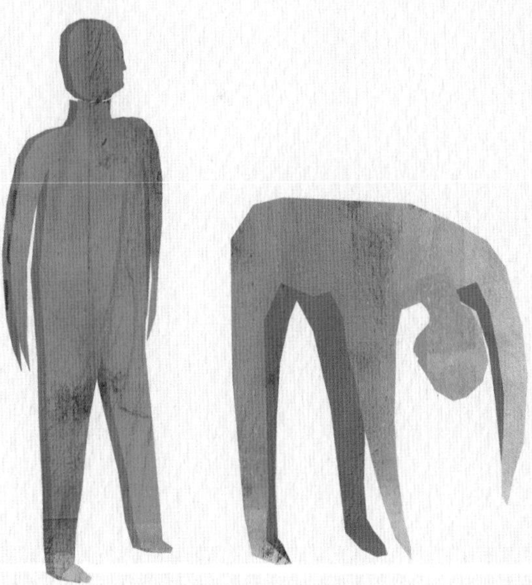

Watch-out points

~ Avoid if you have a disc-related illness.

~ Bend your knees if you have tight hamstrings.

~ Draw the abdominals in as you move forwards and down.

~ When you first try this exercise, start with a half-roll down, and stop when your fingertips touch the thighs above the knees, then return.

~ Slowly increase the range of movement.

~ With the modification, avoid pulling the knee into the chest; let it sink into the chest, and avoid lifting the hips or buttocks.

A Dreaming, Shuniya*

Dew mist is rising with the sun
From the silken rivers of my dreams –
you've been dragging idle fingers and
through rubbed eyes there is a ripple –
just visible. An ever dispersing circle
To catch kinesis of this vapour
I dip the pen into the page
And ink-dyed fly
To tempt memory to bite
And bankside to sacrifice
Its gills to air
But you swim back down deeper,
Cooler down to settle
Camouflaged in the silty shingle
Evading capture
Later I glimpse the trace of you
At the bottom of this page
A blinking cursor pause for thinking
And a comma loose, alone, adrift
That's sprung the catch of syntax
Is wandering free
Just a mis-struck key
A breath to breathe you in
Outside the smother of my airing
And this slack-knotted net of words

SUZANNE PAYLOR

* THE POINT OF STILLNESS

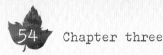

Low mood and procrastination

When low mood takes over, when the blues are in our head and heart, there can be moments and hours and days when life seems almost not worth living. In studying mindfulness, we try to become aware of all that life offers, at the same time realizing that everything is but momentary, and that nothing lasts for ever.

The poem 'The Song of Wandering Aengus' (see page 57) typifies for me how destructive emotions, such as low mood, sadness and worry, can take hold of us. Aengus goes out into nature because his emotions are aflame with negativity. In nature he finds himself and mindfully starts fishing, a pastime that is for many very soothing. His heart starts to feel excitement and joy when he catches a trout, which will serve him as his dinner, or so he thinks. But no sooner has he started the preparation than the fish is transformed into a beautiful maiden, who calls his name, only to disappear within moments. Now Aengus goes down the well-trodden path of attachment, wanting and unfulfilled desire. He searches for the maiden for his entire life, believing that only when he is reunited with her will he know joy and feel he has arrived.

The Song of Wandering Aengus

I went out to the hazel wood,
Because a fire was in my head,
And cut and peeled a hazel wand,
And hooked a berry to a thread;
And when white moths were on the wing,
And moth-like stars were flickering out,
I dropped the berry in a stream
And caught a little silver trout.

When I had laid it on the floor
I went to blow the fire a-flame,
But something rustled on the floor,
And someone called me by my name:
It had become a glimmering girl
With apple blossom in her hair
Who called me by my name and ran
And faded through the brightening air.

Though I am old with wandering
Through hollow lands and hilly lands,
I will find out where she has gone,
And kiss her lips and take her hands;
And walk among long dappled grass,
And pluck till time and times are done
The silver apples of the moon,
The golden apples of the sun.

WILLIAM BUTLER YEATS (1865–1939)

I love Yeat's poem The Song of Wandering Aengus, the language, the metaphors, but I chose it for this chapter's introduction because it is one of the best illustrations of 'the human condition'! We find it so difficult to live in the moment and to enjoy what is. Rather, we follow dreams, expectations and illusions, while our actual life passes us by. What if Aengus never finds her? Will the silver apples of the moon and the golden apples of the sun never be plucked? Will he live his life searching for something that may have only existed in his imagination?

Low mood, if ongoing and persistent, can end up leading to depression, which is very much a growing malaise of the 21st century. In conjunction with the World Health Organization (WHO), World Mental Health (WMH) researchers from 20 centres collaborated to investigate the prevalence of depression around the globe based on detailed interviews with over 89,000 people. The results showed that 15 per cent of the population from high-income countries (compared to 11 per cent for low/middle-income countries) were likely to get depression at least once in their lifetime.

Signs of a major depressive episode include five or more of the following symptoms, lasting for two or more weeks:

- Feeling depressed, in a very low mood, becoming upset for no specific reason
- Suicidal thoughts
- Feelings of guilt, worthlessness, anxiety, irritability
- Loss of interest and pleasure
- Difficulty concentrating
- Sleep disturbance – waking early or sleeping much longer than usual
- Decrease or increase in weight
- General tiredness or upon waking; loss of energy
- Inability to concentrate/indecisiveness

Yeats's poem is a sad tale that many individuals are familiar with, having experienced the emotions themselves or witnessed them in friends and family. Aengus certainly feels anxious, irritable and tired, and takes no interest or pleasure in his real life. His only focus is trying to find his lost love. A dream that touched his reality for less than a few minutes becomes his lifelong obsession.

In a similar way, we procrastinate in our lives. We avoid engaging with the real thing – our life – because subconsciously we want to avoid failing and being alone. So, instead of pursuing something worthwhile and meaningful, we keep writing emails, texting or phoning anybody who comes to mind. If we never finish this 'project', you see, it can never fail.

By becoming mindful of our tendencies to distract ourselves or keep busy all the time, we actually start to engage with the real thing: the experience of every moment, however it may unfold, whether it is joyful, painful or neutral. This is the nature of life, with everything coming and going, starting and finishing. Stepping into your life can simply start by *really* having a shower, eating a meal or listening to the sounds of the wind. It is an invitation to reconnect to this childlike curiosity in order to truly experience the moment as it actually presents itself. Of course, this may sound paradoxical, particularly when we open up to the difficult moments that offer themselves to us. But as they are happening anyway, like it or not, by being really present we may be able to respond wisely to a challenge and thereby reduce the blow that fate has dealt us.

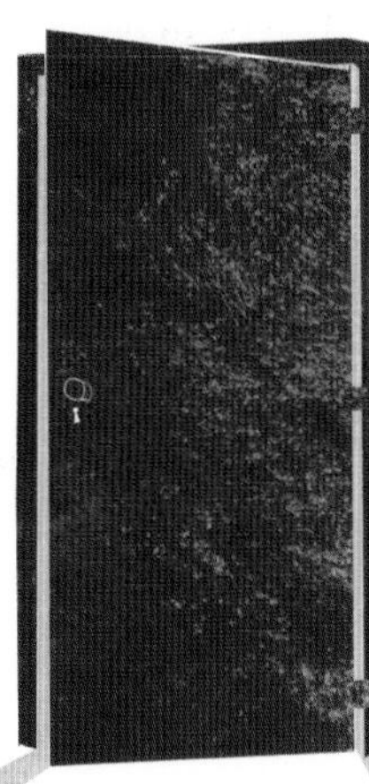

Life will not let you fall

An invitation

Here, writer Rainer Maria Rilke shares his thoughts on welcoming difficult feelings:

We have no reason to mistrust our world, because it surely is not working against us. If it presents us with horrors, they are often the horrors we create with our minds, if there are deep abysses, once more they are ours to deal with and even dangers which are present may be there for us to engage lovingly with. And if we follow the principle that recommends us to live life on the edge of the most difficult, with time, whatever is experienced now as the most challenging, may turn into a trusted, most dear friend. How could we possibly forget the ancient tales of our forefathers. The myths of dragons, who at the last moment turn into princesses. Maybe all dragons that show up during our lives are in fact princesses who desperately wait for the moment which gives them the opportunity to be beautiful and brave. Maybe everything that appears horrific at first is actually, deep down, a helpless thing that deeply yearns for our touch and acceptance.

And even if a sadness arises so deep and never yet experienced, and when anxiety hovers above your light and shadows and all your actions, please do not fear them too much. I would like to remind you that life has not forgotten you. It is holding you by your hand and will not let you fall. Why do you want to shut out of your life any uneasiness or any depression? For after all, even though you do not know now where all of this will lead to, these experiences may lead to the change that you were always hoping for.

From Letters to a Young Poet by Rainer Maria Rilke
adapted by Patrizia Collard

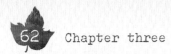

Breathing practices

The formal practices I have selected for dealing with low mood and procrastination can be achieved by most readers. If your body is not able to do them, just sit comfortably and run through them in your mind. Please remember never to do anything that causes pain. Less is often more.

Each time you get ready to practise, take a few moments to 'check in' with yourself. Always feel free to remain in a pose for longer, or to practise only one or two poses, if that feels best to your body.

Breath is life energy. When we restrict our breathing, we diminish our life energy. Without breath, there is no more life. Feeling low is often accompanied by shallow breathing. The yogis knew that it was not always possible to influence emotions and thought processes directly, so their approach became very sophisticated. Via breath and movements, they indirectly influence and control feelings, moods and thoughts. By managing your breath, you can make such a difference to how you feel. As your energy starts to improve, you could experiment with the postures. However, always make sure that you don't strain and push yourself.

This means you can use your breathing and very simple movements to influence how you feel, and slowly you may notice that your mood is ever so slightly lifting. A breath that is energizing and helps you to open up your breathing can also help you to re-energize as a whole and enable you to face the day with more energy and enthusiasm. But please don't put yourself under any pressure to be different from your tired and 'low' self, if that is how you are. What is mostly needed is a kind, forgiving and accepting attitude towards yourself.

When starting your session, take a moment to get closer to your breathing – to 'befriend' it. Is it shallow or deep, slow or fast, smooth or rough, regular or irregular? Do you find yourself sighing often, struggling for breath? Do you tend to push it or hold it? Is the count between the inhalation and the exhalation the same or is one longer than the other? If you explore your breathing with this curiosity and open questioning, you will get a good insight into where you are right now. It is from this baseline that you can notice any differences. Is your breathing forced or natural? Are you rushing it, holding it, pushing it? Does the in-breath dominate your breathing? Are you gasping for breath, or is the out-breath dominant? This may even help you to find out what restored the energy you were lacking. If you continue this process of 'watching your breathing', you may experience a more energetic self and achieve joy and a zest for life again.

Practice: Feeling your breath

1 Sit comfortably on a chair or lie on your back. You can bend your knees, feet on the floor, or put a bolster under your knees, or extend the legs a little bit more than hip-width apart.

2 With your left palm on your belly, place your right hand:

- beneath the left collarbone – keep it here and feel the breath;
- into the left armpit – keep it here and feel the breath.

3 Now change sides. Make soft fists and place them just below the sternum, and then place the palms softly at the side of the ribcage, on the belly and in the groin area, where the thighs meet the pelvis.

4 Experience and feel your breathing.

Practice: Gentle chest opener

1 Roll up a bath towel and place it lengthways on your blanket or yoga mat. Sit with your buttocks on the end of it and then, supporting yourself with your arms, lower your spine over the rolled-up towel. Make sure you are resting on the entire towel, from the tailbone to the top of the head.

2 The arms are by your side, either close to the body or touching the outer edge of the mat, or even extended to make a T-shape. Your legs are bent or stretched; you can have a rolled-up blanket under your knees to support the back of your legs. Relax the legs so they fall open. If your head tilts backwards and your neck feels tight, place a pillow under your head.

3 You are now opening your chest and this can help you to enhance your breathing. It will also help you very gently and compassionately to reverse the close-down posture that often goes along with low mood. Stay here for 5–15 minutes.

4 To finish, roll over onto your side, moving the towel to the side. Finally, roll over onto your back again and feel any sensations in your back and chest.

Watch-out points

~ Avoid tensing your body – pay particular attention to your neck and shoulders.

~ You can also place your hands gently on the stomach, or spread them out wide if more comfortable.

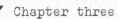

Practice: Shoulder bridge

1 Lie on your back, with the legs bent at the knees, the feet and knees hip-width apart, the ankles below the knees, and the feet firmly grounded and evenly weighted on the floor. Place your arms by your side, with the palms facing down.

2 Breathe out, tuck the tailbone under and then lift the buttocks, then the lower back, vertebra by vertebra, peel the spine off the ground. The weight of the body is resting on your feet and, in the end position, on the shoulders and head as well. Keep the neck long; avoid lifting the chin away from the chest. Return to the start position on the inhalation.

3 Repeat this 5 times.

Practice: Spinal rotation

1 Place your legs and feet as in Shoulder bridge, but now stretch your arms to the sides into a V-shape or even further up to shoulder level into a T-shape.

2 Inhaling and exhaling slowly, lower your knees to the right, with the buttocks following; the movement continues through your spine, like a corkscrew turning. Towards the end of the movement, turn the head to the left. Holding the position, inhale, and on the exhalation return to the centre position. Inhale, then exhale and repeat on the other side. Remember: only move with the exhalation; hold with the inhalation.

3 Repeat this 3 times on each side. On the last repetition, and only if you feel comfortable, hold for 4–6 breaths and, with each exhalation, sink deeper into the position.

Practice: Knees into chest

1 Bend your legs, one after the other, into the chest and gently hold them, but avoid pulling them, into the chest. Keep your spine long as you press each vertebra into the floor, and avoid hunching the shoulders up. If you struggle to hug your legs, hold them behind the knees.

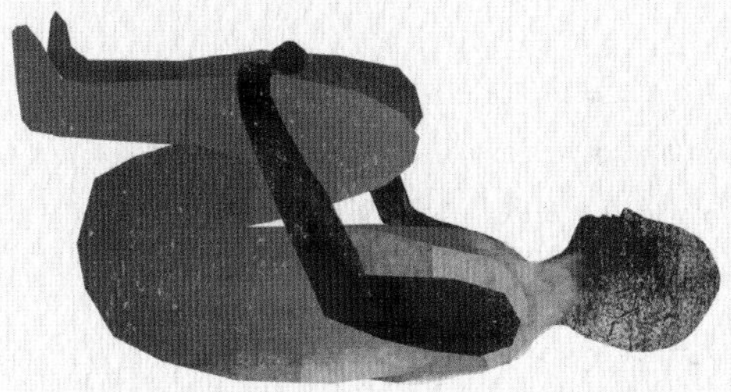

Practice: Relaxation

1 Lying on your back with arms by your sides and the palms of your hands facing the ceiling, cover yourself with a thin blanket and rest for ten minutes; feel the physical sensations that are in your body and the breathing that is moving in and out of your body.

2 Slowly come up and check in with your body. How is your breathing now compared to the beginning of the session? Do you notice any difference in body and mind? Is your energy level the same or has it decreased – you might have done too much too early? Does your mind feel still or restless? Whatever it feels like, that is okay.

Ever Changing

Life is ever changing,
There are endings and new beginnings,
Keeping hopes, keeping hopes alive.

And like evolution,
Change is a solution,
Changing, changing to survive.

And we know,
Know that change can bring
Sorrows,
Poisoning everything.
And wise heads say,
We should try to accept what we cannot change.
And wise heads say,
We should try to accept what we cannot change.

Change is time in motion,
Heading in one direction,
As we grow, learn and strive,
Changing, changing to survive.

SONG LYRICS BY ANN-MARIE GILKES

Illness and loss

Illness can really take over one's life, whether it is a short-lived and intense illness, a potentially incurable and chronic one, or one that when it is healed requires you to adapt to a totally new way of being alive. Mindfulness teachings encourage us to accept first what is here, even if we really don't want it.

Then we are encouraged to respond mindfully to the experience, with wisdom and patience. Of course, this attitude is very hard to apply when you are dealing with a long-term illness or the loss of mobility, a limb or your looks due to an accident or a fire. The list goes on and on.

I have, however, learned the lesson that acceptance may help us not merely to exist due to our illness but to learn to live around it and with it, and settle into a meaningful life as best as we can. The only thing we know for sure is that everything changes all the time. Even with incurable diseases or the loss of our previously functioning body, there is still change. What kind of change and when it will take place – we simply do not know. We just have to be patient.

A mindful approach

Norman Cousins, an American journalist who became seriously sick and partially paralysed with a rare disease, cured himself through self-compassion, large dosages of vitamin C and laughter therapy. He was told he had only a few months to live, but he wrote in *Anatomy of an Illness*, 'Since I did not accept the verdict, I wasn't trapped in the cycle of fear, depression and panic that frequently 'accompanies' a supposedly incurable illness.'

A close friend of mine broke her neck in a motorcycle accident when she was 18. Although she can barely move her hands and can only feel her body from her shoulders upwards, she nevertheless has a real life – I mean one that is purposeful because she chose to make it so. She is such an inspiration. She is a therapist and meditation teacher, and her whole attitude of acceptance is an inspiration for her clients. She works not only with others who have experienced spinal injuries, but also with anybody who cares to make an appointment with her. Initially, she always tells her clients what happened to her 30 years ago and then she goes on to say, 'So now that is out of the way, kindly tell me why you have decided to start therapy.'

I still get frustrated, and forget about being mindful and patient, when the two of us decide to go to see a film on the spur of the moment and are told on our arrival at the cinema that the only disabled space has already been sold. It is suggested that we come back for the late-night viewing. I want to argue that we could sit at the back or on the side of a row with the wheelchair in the aisle but, of course, this is never possible because of fire regulations. This is a recurrent experience in restaurants, cinemas, theatres and so on. At moments like this, my friend is much more able to access mindfulness than I am. She just smiles (acceptance) and says, 'Let's go to my place, get a hugely unhealthy take-away and watch Charlie Chaplin' (wise response rather than fuming reaction). She is so calm and has accepted her new body, where legs have been replaced by wheels. For me, she personifies mindfulness!

Taking a mindful approach to illness and loss means initially accepting what is, and then bit by bit seeing how you can regain some control over your life, rather than letting the diagnosis label you. None of us knows how much lifetime we have left. Therefore it makes sense (for me at least) to savour each moment, to truly live right here, right now.

There is the story of the 'two arrows' that the Buddha told to his visitors. Life often shoots an arrow at you and wounds you. However, by not accepting what has happened, by worrying about it, by saying it is unfair and wondering how long the pain will last, we tend to shoot a second arrow into the open wound and increase and prolong the pain. Pain is often a given, but suffering is optional.

Mindfulness teaches us that each moment is a new beginning and that we indeed do not know how the wind will turn. The mindfulness practice that I recommend in this chapter is called the Body Scan. It endeavours to show you that usually there is more right with you than wrong.

Practice: Body scan meditation

This practice is particularly useful for getting in touch with our whole sensory experience. With this practice, we gradually travel through our body, to the areas we are less aware of, to the ones we do know, and to the others that may cause problems or pain. By truly opening up to this experience – this journey through the 'within' – we learn to understand what our body is trying to say to us and also that not every part is broken. It can help us to create a healthy relationship with a body that we deem imperfect. This is the house we live in and it is all we have. So it may be helpful to learn to accept it and make the most of it.

1 Make yourself comfortable in a room where you will not be disturbed and where you will be warm. Lie on your back on a mat or rug on the floor or on your bed. Allow your eyes to close gently.

2 Take a few moments to get in touch with the movement of your breath and the sensations in your body. When you are ready, bring your awareness to the physical sensations in your body, especially touch, where your body is in contact with the floor or the bed. On each out-breath, allow yourself to let go, sinking a little deeper into the mat or bed.

Monks meditating in corpse position.

3 Remind yourself of the intention of this practice. Its aim is not to feel any different, relaxed or calm; this may or may not happen. Instead, the intention of the practice is, as best you can, to bring awareness to any sensations you detect, as you are attending to each part of the body in turn.

4 Now bring your awareness to the physical sensations in the lower abdomen, bringing awareness to the changing sensations in the abdominal wall as you breathe in, and as you breathe out. Take a few minutes to feel the sensations as you breathe in and as you breathe out. It may be helpful to put your hand on your belly and to really feel each breath as it comes in and as it leaves the body, noticing that some may be deeper, others shallower, and that there tends to be a little pause between each in- and out-breath.

5 Having connected with the sensations in the abdomen, bring your focus gently down the left leg, into the left foot. Focus on each of the toes of the left foot in turn – the big toe, the little toe and the toes in between. Bring a gentle curiosity even to the spaces between the toes: feel them, sense them or simply know that they are there. Perhaps notice the sense of tingling or warmth, or no particular sensation. Now broaden your field of awareness to the rest of the left foot: the sole, the heel, the upper part, the little bones and blood vessels, the ankle, and even the skin covering the foot. Then continue to move your awareness further up your left leg, to: the calf, the shin, the knee, the thigh.

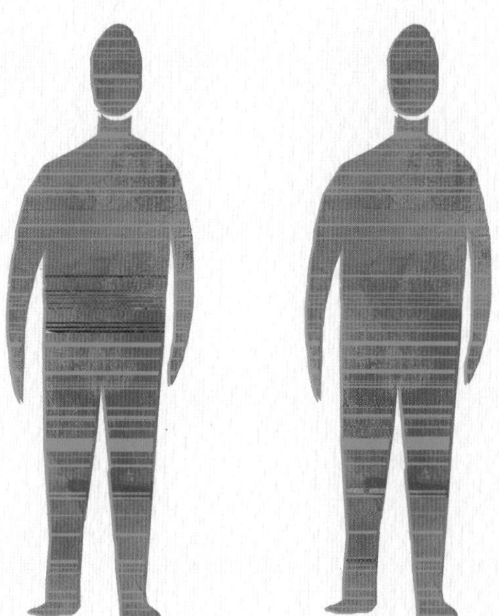
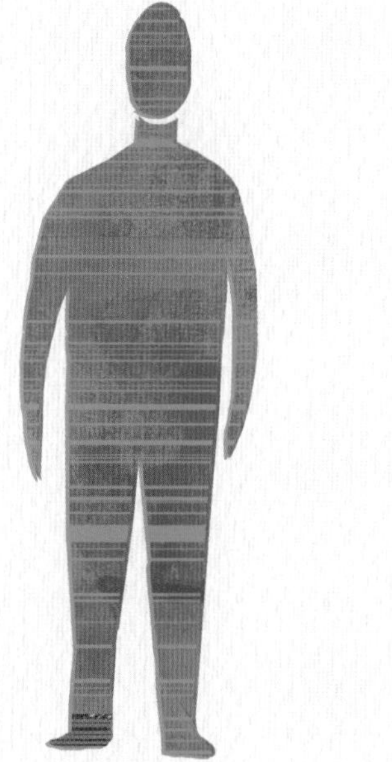
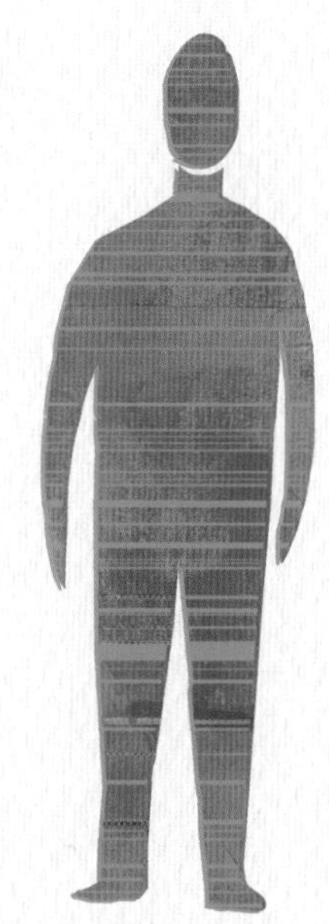

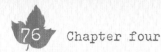

6 When you are ready, on an in-breath, feel the breath entering the nostrils, then the lungs, and then passing down into the abdomen, the left leg and the left foot. Then, on the out-breath, feel or imagine the breath coming all the way back up, out of the foot, into the leg, up through the abdomen and chest, and out through the nose. On each out-breath, have a sense of releasing any tension or discomfort. As best you can, continue this for a few breaths, breathing down into the toes, and back out from the toes. It may be an unusual thing to do, but with the help of our intention it may become easier and easier; just practise this 'breathing into', approaching it playfully, with the curiosity of a child.

7 Continue to bring awareness, and a gentle curiosity, to the physical sensations in each part of the rest of the body in turn: right toes, right foot, right leg, pelvic area, back, abdomen, chest, fingers, hands, arms, shoulders, neck, head and face. In each area, as best as you can, bring the same gentle curiosity to the bodily sensations that are present. As you leave each major area, 'breathe into it' on the in-breath, and let go of that region on the out-breath.

8 Remember that when you become aware of any tension or other intense sensation in a particular part of the body, 'breathe into it' and, as best as you can, have a sense of letting go or releasing on the out-breath.

9 The mind will, without doubt, wander away from the breath and the body from time to time. That is entirely normal – it is what our minds tend to do. When this happens, gently acknowledge it, noticing where the mind has gone off to. Then, gently return your awareness to the part of the body where you intended your focus to be.

10 After 'scanning' the whole body in this way, spend a few minutes being aware of a sense of the body as a whole, and of the breath flowing freely in and out of the body.

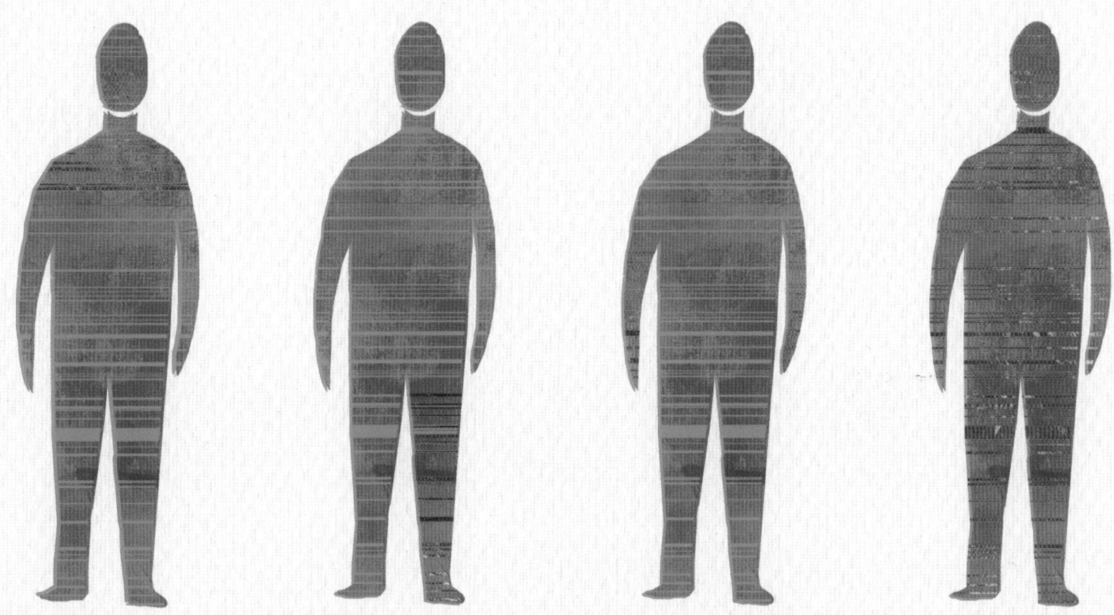

Watch-out points

~ Should you notice yourself falling asleep, prop your head up with a pillow or open your eyes and continue the practice this way, remembering that the intention of the body scan is to fall awake to the experience of being alive in this body. There is no need to feel guilty, though, should sleep envelop you. This may just mean that you are really tired and need sleep (compassion), which is truly okay. Each body scan is a new beginning.

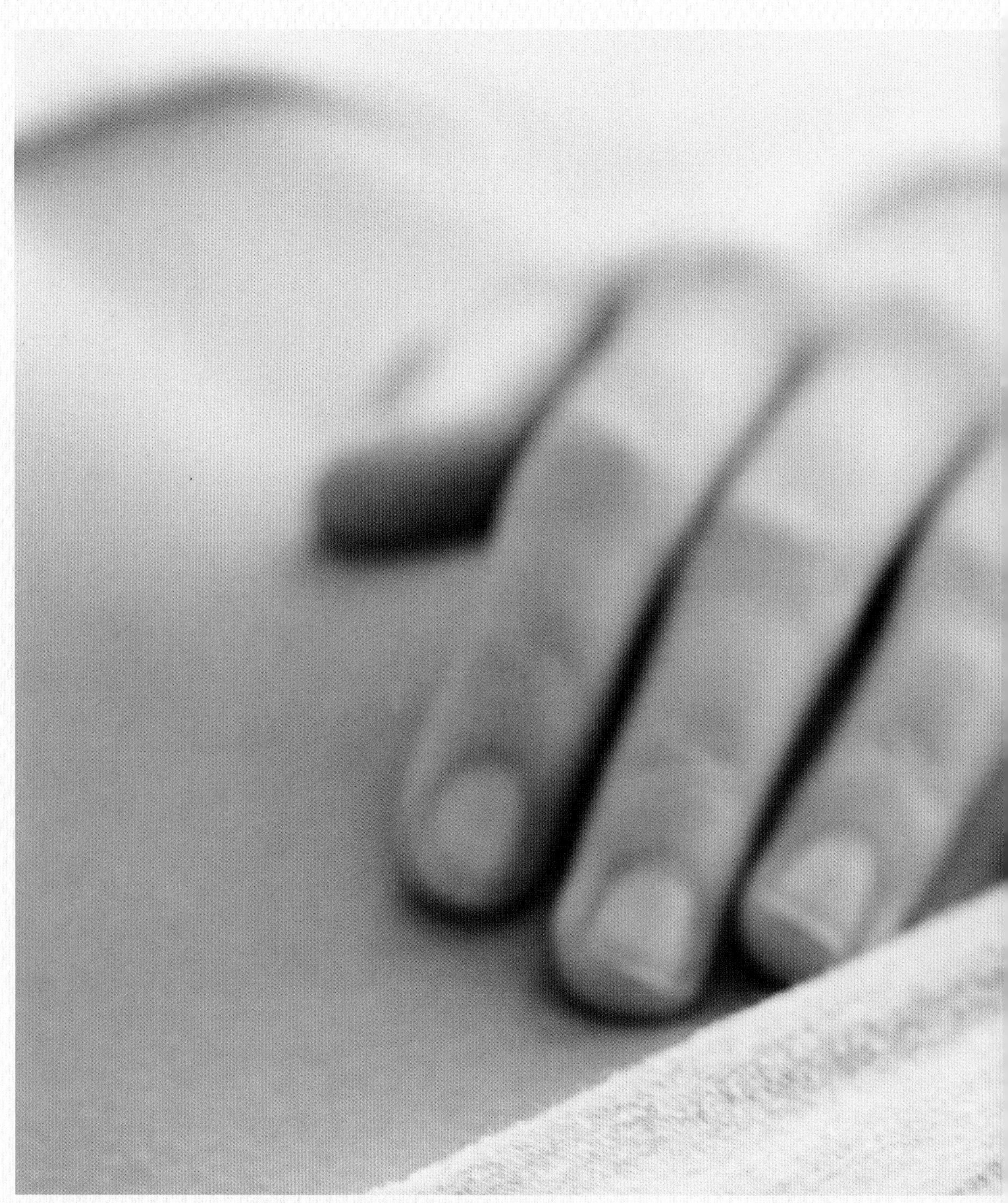

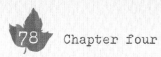

Practice: Mindful breathing

There are times when we are so ill that the idea of moving the body makes us crunch. If this is the case, allow yourself to stay in bed, relaxing and being with your breath; just observing and feeling it will be enough. I think this is a good moment to experience how important breathing is because, even if we don't feel like moving, the breath is still flowing in and out of the body and sustaining all our bodily functions. We are not normally aware of the importance of breathing because it is just there, it comes free and mostly we take it for granted.

Here are some mindful breathing exercises for when you feel ill.

1 Lie on your back with your legs stretched out and allow yourself to be totally relaxed. Alternatively, you may want to sit in a comfortable position, using pillows, if you wish, for support.

2 When you are inhaling, open your toes like a flower opening to the sunshine. Do, please, use your imagination. When you are exhaling, scrunch your toes as if the flower is closing. If you tend to get cramps, do the closing action very gently.

3 When you are inhaling, softly point your toes away from you, and when you are exhaling, flex your feet to bring them perpendicular to the floor.

4 Curl the ankles in each direction, clockwise and anticlockwise.

Watch-out points

~ The simple co-ordination of breath and movement will slowly bring back some energy and may help you to start moving again. When you get up, you can incorporate simple tasks, such as going to the bathroom, getting dressed, making a cup of tea, and so on, mindfully. Mindful walking also comes very naturally after we have been ill. Each step at a time restores the wondrous gift of walking.

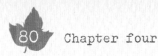

5 Bring one leg to tabletop position (thigh resting in the hip joint, perpendicular to the ground, and the calf parallel to the floor as if it is resting on a coffee table; the knee is bending at 90°). When you are inhaling, open the knee and extend the leg towards the ceiling. When you are exhaling, fold it back to the tabletop position. Change sides after 6–9 repetitions.

6 Now slide the feet in, bringing them closer to the buttocks, one after the other, and rest the feet on the floor, hip-width apart. When you are inhaling, drop/open the knees to the side, and when you are exhaling, bring the knees back up.

7 Open the arms to the side, either to a V-shape or a T-shape. When you are exhaling, drop both the knees to the right; the hips, pelvis, lower back and spine will follow this movement, with the head staying soft in the centre or turning slightly to the left. During the inhalation, hold the position. When the exhalation begins, return the spine, pelvis, hips and knees back to the start position. Repeat on the other side. Remember that you are moving when you are exhaling, and staying in the position when you are inhaling.

8 Now relax your legs by stretching them away from you. If this is uncomfortable, stay in the previous position. With the arms along the sides of your body, bend them at the elbow to bring the forearms perpendicular to the floor. Turn the palms to face the front (same direction as your toes). When you are inhaling, open and gently spread your fingers wide; when you are exhaling tuck the thumb into the palm first and squeeze the other four fingers into a fist. Repeat to the rhythm of the breathing. Do this 6–9 times more.

9 Keep your arms and palms in the same position. Now, moving from the wrist and with the inhalation, point the hand and fingers forwards and then down to the floor. When you are exhaling, change the direction, flex at the wrist and hand, and your fingers will point in the direction of the head.

10 Make a fist with the thumb in the palm; gently squeeze it with the four fingers and make circles. After 6–9 repetitions, change direction.

Practice: Loss

How can we be in a wise relationship with pain, fear and loss? There is no simple answer that fits all. What I find useful, and therefore will share with you, is to simply sit with what is. Don't try to change it, to wish it away or to 'fast forward'. Every moment is what it is; every moment passes at last. Being with 'what is' is perhaps the most fundamental mindfulness practice, and yet the most challenging for a 'quick-fix' society.

Sit in a dignified, upright posture in a room where you won't be disturbed. Feel your feet firmly grounded on the floor, your back aligned with your neck and your hands resting in your lap – make sure you feel comfortable.

1 Start the practice with a gentle focus on your breathing. Allow each in-breath to enter your body and expand for its full duration – don't force anything, just allow your body to breathe itself. Then, after a natural break, breathe out the out-breath for its full duration, until it comes to a natural end. Do this for a while, as long as it takes to feel settled enough. Then focus on the 'loss' – it may be health, a friendship or partnership, or even the death of somebody close to you. Gently say to yourself: 'Whatever it is (here you fill in the 'loss' either verbally or as an image) let me feel it.' So, for example: 'My beloved ________ who has left me (or been called away – use your own words), I am sitting here and am prepared to feel the pain of this loss.' Start gently with a very simple phrase or image and just hold this in your awareness. Be with it, feeling, seeing the loss, facing it, even if it is painful, but don't pretend it is not there. You may only be able to do this for a minute or two.

2 Then let go of the thought or image, and return to the simple breath of life.

Peace

There is only silence
On the mountain tops
Among the tips of the trees
You perceive barely a breath
Even the birds in the forest
Keep still and are silent
Wait then
Just a little while longer
And you too
will find peace at last.

J.W. von Goethe
(translated by Patrizia Collard)

Cultivating older age

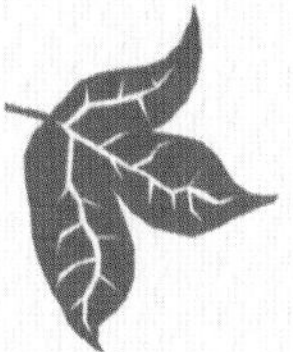

Mindfulness is being aware of, or bringing attention to, this moment in time, on purpose and with intention. So when we go for a mindful walk and really notice every little detail around us – trees, cars, little flowers growing out of small cracks, a pretty cat crossing the road – rather than creating 'To Do Lists', we may feel truly enchanted with life.

When I think of older age, I feel trepidation and/or excitement – it all depends on my state of mind. Trepidation appears in the foreground of my awareness whenever I see a large number of old people sitting in a room, watching either television inside or the world outside, as if life was no longer happening to them. I experienced this a few years back while on a retreat entitled 'Being with Suffering' that took place in a nursing home. Only a very few of the residents ever ventured outside, and then only for a couple of minutes or so at a time; they looked very frightened and frail.

Whenever I meet old people, I am amazed at the stories they have to tell. There was Charlie, who, at the time of chatting me up while I was on a sightseeing tour in Berlin, was 96 years old. I explained to him that I needed to catch up with my group and also that my man Bernhard was part of that group. Although Charlie was perhaps a little disappointed, he told me of a Kaffeehaus where he would wait for both of us when the tour was finished. I am so grateful that he did just that. That afternoon a wonderful friendship began, one that lasted for seven years until Charlie died at the age of 103. He showed us Berlin from a new point of view because, unlike president J F Kennedy, he was a real Berliner. He showed us many hidden spots known only to locals. He told us about his life in the silent black-and-white film industry and how, during the Second World War, he had emigrated to South America and made movies there. He told us much, much more – I could write a whole chapter or even a book about Charlie. He had suffered from prostate cancer when he was in his 60s, but did not feel like dying then, particularly as he was nursing his bedridden wife, who needed him. He recovered and looked after her without any help until she passed away. Charlie was sad about some things, but mainly he was passionate about life and being alive. One of his favourite activities was going to the airport and mindfully watching people; perhaps he was still making movies in his mind.

Another friend of mine, Stella, at the age of 86, swims several times each week at 6 o'clock in the morning, meditates, goes to the theatre and cinema, and teaches a free yoga class for an over-60s club. Every class ends with a meditation practice. She recently flew to New York for a couple of weeks on her own. She travels a lot on overland buses, for 24 hours, visiting Paris, Rome and Vienna, or wherever else takes her fancy. She once told me that 'getting old is not a doddle', but she is making a pretty adventurous thing out of it.

Ageing mindfully

So, moving on from the personal, let us briefly look at a few others who live, or have lived, life moment by moment and to the full.

- Nelson Mandela (1918–) became president of South Africa in 1994 after 27 years of imprisonment. He continues to support a number of good causes.

- Viktor Frankl (1905–1997) survived three concentration camps – Theresienstadt, Dachau and Auschwitz – and turned down the opportunity to escape in order to remain with the inmates who had become his 'patients'. He decided to stay with the 'search for meaning', which was based on his belief that we all have the freedom to determine our purpose and thus our well-being. Frankl developed and practised Logotherapy, a form of psychotherapy, and lived into his 90s.

- Grandma Moses (1860–1961) started painting when she was in her late 70s after the death of her husband. She became a world-renowned 'naive' painter and very wealthy, too, although this was not her motivation. She lived to be 101 years old.

- Hans Hass (1919–), who invented scuba diving and pioneered underwater photography, continued to dive right up to the age of 89.

The importance of having meaning in your life

Let me also mention the famous centenarians of Okinawa, Japan, who live on the 'island of long life'. Their longevity is at least partially due to practising prayer and meditation and holding each moment as something valuable in their awareness. They simply enjoy being alive. And so the circle that starts with the simple joy of the adventure of life in childhood closes also with that same possibility. There need not be a greater purpose than this.

I would also like to mention two people who deeply influenced the world by being living examples of mindfulness and loving kindness, ambassadors for peace and reconciliation. Thich Nhat Hanh and the Dalai Lama, who are responsible for inspiring generations, both had to leave their homelands (Vietnam and Tibet, respectively) in order to continue their work. But by closing this door, another one opened for them, and they achieved amazing things by spreading a message that is thousands of years old.

Thich Nhat Hanh (1926–) created the Order of Interbeing in 1966, and established a beautiful retreat centre called Plum Village near Bordeaux, France. He heads a monastic and lay group, teaching mindfulness trainings. He still travels the world, writes books – and smiles. Meanwhile, Tenzin Gyatso, His Holiness the 14th Dalai Lama (1935–), the youngest of them all, perhaps needs no introduction, but just a few words from him: 'My message is Love!' So what do all these people have in common? What is the common denominator that kept them 'using it rather than losing it'?

They had meaning in their life and an innate wish to actualize their purpose. Frankl says in his book *The Doctor and the Soul*: 'This will-to-meaning is the most human phenomenon of all, which we do not seem to share with any other being on earth.' Moment-to-moment real living – tasting life, not just staying alive, but savouring any opportunity life offers us – seems to make life worth living for a hundred years or more.

There is a lovely book by Father Anselm Grün, the Benedictine monk, entitled *The Art of Growing Older*. A particular metaphor held in a story within it touched me deeply, which I would like to share it with you. Ageing can be compared to the four seasons. Spring symbolizes childhood and youth. Summer then shines brightly as an independent adult, who can, if s/he chooses, create a life full of adventure. Autumn, on the other hand, creates new colours and smells in nature, when the sun is shining less harshly and rather more kindly. This is the time for harvesting and reaping, but also for trying new things, now that one may have fewer responsibilities, such as bringing up children or making a career. Winter has its own beauty. There is peace, quiet and an invitation to slow down one's pace, yet it is filled with possibilities – building snowmen outside or sitting in front of an open fire inside, telling stories or simply 'being alive'.

'The Warmth of the Heart Prevents Your Body from Rusting' is a song sung every day by the people of Okinawa

QUOTED FROM MARIE DE HENNEZEL'S 2008 BOOK OF THE SAME NAME

Practice: Be with the breath

Find a spot in your home where you will feel peaceful and be left undisturbed. You can sit on a chair or on the floor; leaning against a wall to support your spine is a wonderful way, too. Make sure you keep warm, so perhaps wrap a shawl or a blanket round you. You may wish to light a candle.

1 Sit in a comfortable upright posture and feel a sense of dignity. Let your shoulders drop and soften your facial muscles.

2 Close your eyes, if this feels comfortable, or keep them in soft focus.

3 Bring your awareness to your body sensations, by focusing your attention on the sensations of touch where your body makes contact with the floor or whatever you are sitting on. Spend a few minutes exploring these sensations. Simply feel into your body and let it breathe itself.

4 Bring your attention to your chest and belly, feeling them rise or expand gently on the in-breath and fall or deflate on the out-breath.

5 Keep your attention on your breathing, 'being with' each in-breath for its full duration and with each out-breath for its full duration, as if you were riding the waves of your own breathing. Sooner or later, you may even notice that there is a short pause after the in-breath and the out-breath, and also that each breath seems to have a life of its own and thus differs from any other breath. It is a total moment-to-moment experience when you sit with your breathing.

6 You may notice time and again that the mind has a tendency to wander off – thinking, daydreaming, planning or remembering. At those moments, we will have lost touch with our breathing but that is absolutely okay. Simply notice calmly what it was that took you away from focusing on your breathing and then, gently and without judgement, escort your focus back to your belly and the feeling of the breath coming in and out. It reminds me of

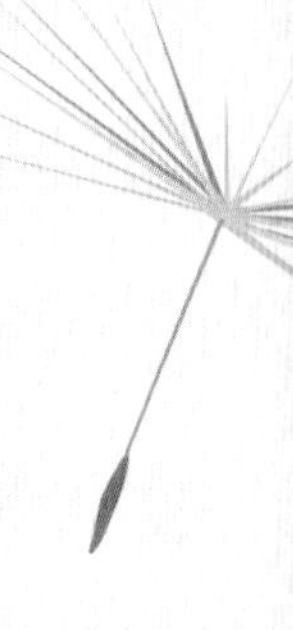

trying gently to rein in a wild horse and train it to be ridden with a saddle and not to run off and hurt itself. The training is gentle, kind and ongoing. Who would ever want to break this beautiful wild horse? Taming it with kindness and without breaking its spirit is the aspiration.

7 Even if you have a mind that likes travelling away from the breath a thousand times or more, all you need do is simply bring it back to the breath every time, no matter what it becomes preoccupied with. It is just as valuable to become aware that your mind has wandered and bring it back to the breath as it is to remain aware of the breath. After all, only a person being mindful will ever notice the wandering nature of the mind.

Watch-out points

- You may want to experiment with different lengths of 'being with the breath'. Maybe start with a few minutes, then see how it goes.
- Try being with the breath at different times of the day – certain times may suit you better.

Case study

Ellen Langer, a well-known psychology researcher into mindfulness, carried out an experiment in a nursing home in Connecticut. A group of residents was given a few mindful everyday activities to add to their daily routines of 'being looked after'. They were encouraged to water a houseplant and make a cup of tea, or make some other small decision in their daily life. Some 18 months later, the people in the group had increased their cheerfulness, alertness and activity levels in comparison to the other residents, and fewer of them had died. This outcome inspired Langer to start a ten-year project on the effects that mindfulness versus mindlessness have on ageing.

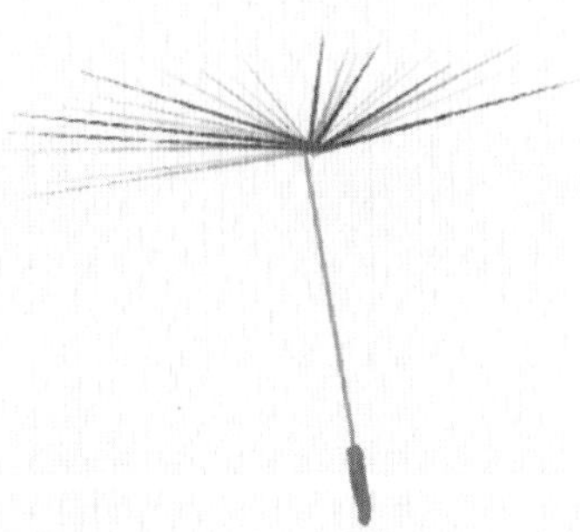

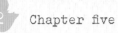

Practice: Palms press

This chair exercise activates the pelvic floor muscles and back muscles, and also helps to lengthen the spine.

1 Sit on a box or a chair without the use of your arms. Keep the feet parallel on the floor, with the hips and knees at a 90° angle and the palms resting on your thighs, pointing towards the knees.

2 Inhale, and as you exhale, draw the navel to your spine, at the same time pressing your palms down on your thighs. This will help you to activate your pelvic floor muscles and support you in lengthening the spine towards the ceiling.

3 Repeat 3–6 times.

Watch-out points

- Keep your shoulders relaxed; avoid hunching them up.
- Apply equal pressure on your palms.

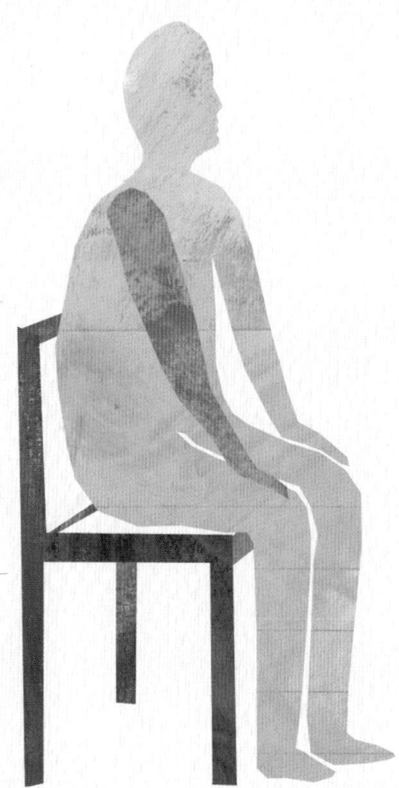

Practice: Wood cutter

This chair exercise helps to strengthen the deep back muscles, especially in the lower back.

1 Sit on a chair, feet hip-width apart, with the hips and knees at a 90° angle. Bend your arms at right angles with your elbows touching the waist. Have the palms facing each other, the hands and fingers actively stretched, and the thumbs touching the palms. You can also do this standing, but make sure your knees are unlocked (gently bent).

2 Move your arms quickly up and down, as if you are making small cutting movements.

3 Continue for 20–30 seconds.

Watch-out points

- Be mindful of where you position yourself to avoid hitting anything.
- Movements should be quick but controlled; lashing out too wildly may cause damage.

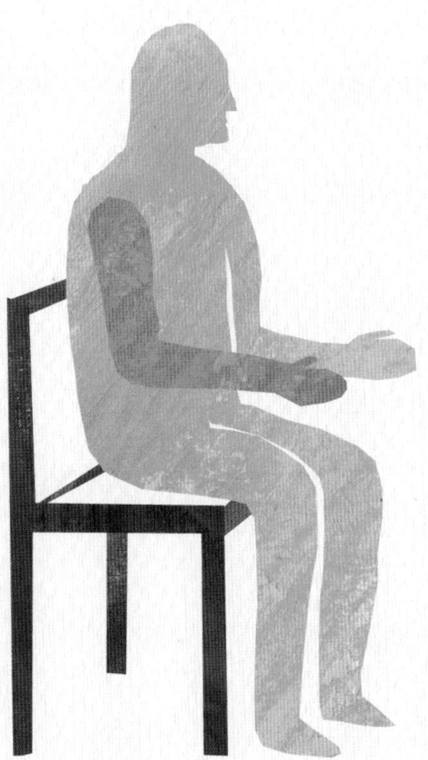

Practice: Side reach/Wind chime

Stretches the sides of the trunk and helps to keep the spine mobile.

1 Sit on a box or a chair, legs hip-width apart, feet parallel, with 90° angles at the hips and knees. Dangle your arms at your side, facing the body. Lengthen the spine and draw in the navel to the spine, engaging the pelvic floor.

2 Inhale, and when exhaling lengthen the spine, at the same time drawing the abdominals to the spine from the front, sides and the back. Keeping it slow and controlled, start to bend to your left side, holding the head in line with the spine. You will notice a light stretch on the right side of your trunk as you are moving towards the left. On your next inhalation, expand your chest and return to the start position. Repeat this movement on the other side.

3 Do this 6 times on each side.

Practice: Chest opener/Dumb waiter

Helps deepen the breathing, opens the chest, reverses hunched-forward shoulders and helps you to feel the correct alignment of the shoulders.

1 Sit on a box or a chair. With your arms by your side, bend your elbows to a 90° angle and tuck them into the waist. Keep them here and turn the palms to face upwards. The tips of the little fingers are nearly touching.

2 Squeeze your shoulder blades together. Your arms will open to the side. Feel the chest opening and then return your palms to the start position.

3 Do this 6 times.

Watch-out points

- Make sure the head and neck stay in line with the spine.
- Avoid leaning forwards.
- Avoid twisting, and keep your hips facing forwards.
- Imagine you are performing the move in between two walls; this will help you to bend without twisting.

Watch-out points

- Keep the elbows tucked into the waist all the time.
- Keep your spine long and supported.
- Your head is resting lightly on the neck, like a helium balloon floating on top of the neck.
- Keep the neck long, and relaxed, with the eyes looking straight ahead.

Practice: Spinal twist/Vine

Spinal rotations keep the spine strong and flexible. This move stretches and strengthens the deep back muscles in the neck and chest.

1 Sit upright on a chair, with your feet hip-width apart, and your spine and neck lengthened upwards. Engage your pelvic floor and draw in the navel to the spine. Relax the shoulders and 'float' the head on top of the neck.

2 Inhale, and when you are exhaling, turn the upper body to the right. At the same time, move the right arm up and behind you, with the eyes following the movement of the right hand, and the head following the movement of the eyes. Move the left palm to the right thigh and touch it by the top and side of the knee. Hold for a count of 3 and then return to the start position. Repeat on the other side.

3 Repeat 3–5 times.

4 If you have a shoulder injury, twist only with your spine. Place your hands in the 'prayer' position, with your palms together and the thumbs touching the breastbone. Keeping your nose, chin and breastbone in one line, rotate the spine.

Caution

If you have a disc-related injury, consult your doctor before doing this move.

Watch-out points

- Keep your hips still and your bodyweight even on both feet and on the buttocks.
- Relax your shoulders.
- Remember always to lengthen your entire spine before you twist.
- Start with a small movement and slowly increase the range.

Practice: Seated forward bend/Charioteer

Stretches the entire back muscles, relieves tension in the back muscles, and helps you to relax.

1 Sit on a chair, with legs slightly wider than hip-width apart, spine lengthened, pelvic floor and abdominals gently engaged, and palms on thighs.

2 Inhale, and when exhaling, 'hinge' forward with your hips. Place your forearms on your thighs with the hands dangling between the legs. Look down between your legs. Keep your shoulders relaxed and notice that your back muscles are working to hold the spine against the pull of gravity, and the abdominals are working to keep the lower back long. Hold here for a count of 5, then return to the start position and repeat 3 more times.

3 Alternatively, sit upright with your hands on the thighs and lengthen your spine. Exhaling, roll your chin to the chest and continue rolling forwards and down, vertebra by vertebra, until you can rest your belly on the thighs. Your arms are dangling along the side of your legs and your palms are facing backwards. Relax the head. Breathe deeply into the sides and back of your ribcage.

4 Hold for a count of 5, then return. You can use your hands and place your palms on your thighs to help you come up again.

Caution

~ If you have a disc-related illness, consult your doctor before doing this move. If you feel uncomfortable, stop and try the alternative version, which is the easier option.

For the First Time

Imagine one day
Really waking up

And just seeing it all
As if for the first time

And just hearing it all
As if for the first time

And smelling, tasting and touching it all
As if for the first time

Allowing joy, amazement and most of all
Gratitude to arise

Stepping into life
As if for the first time

PATRIZIA COLLARD

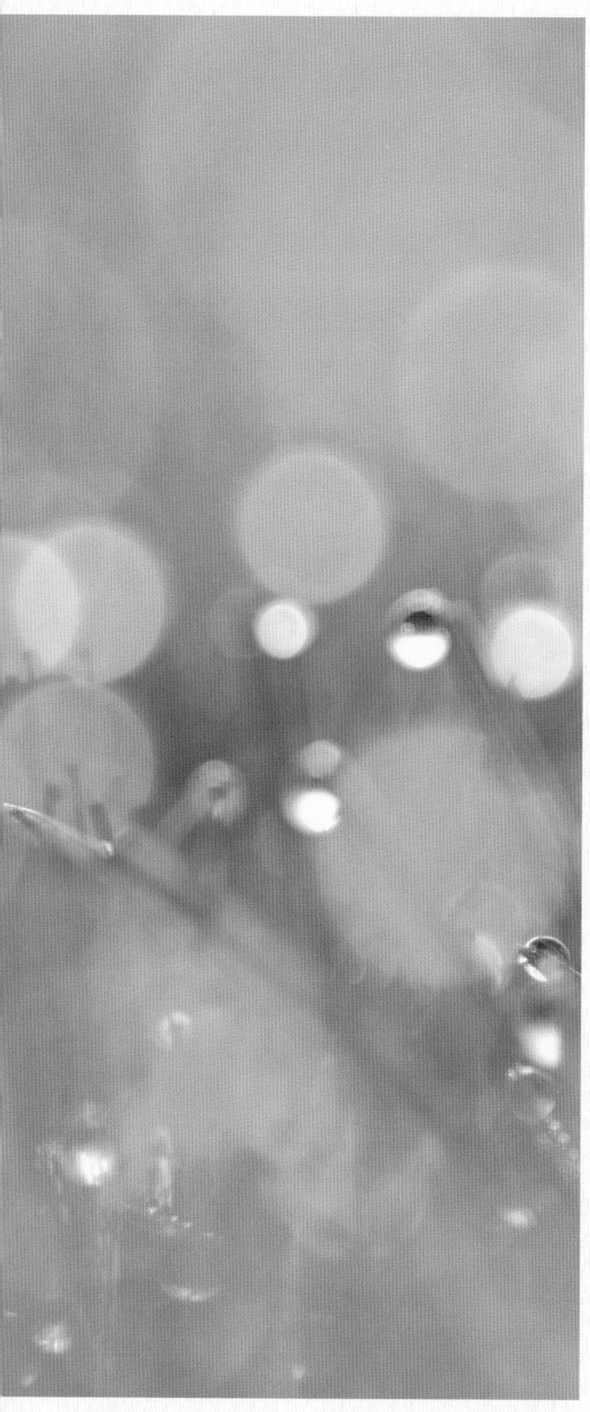

Practice: Everyday mindfulness

In this exercise, the invitation is to pick as a focus of awareness a new aspect of life, to which you have previously not paid much attention. You may choose just ten minutes or so to really look at a particular leaf on a tree, for example, or a stone or a flower or a plant. You may want to think about a piece of furniture or decoration you like, wondering how it came into being and how many people were involved in its creation.

It is my belief that life is precious and can be wonderful. Each moment has a different flavour, but even the bitter ones often enhance our insight and understanding of life. We don't know how long we may walk this earth and breathe the air. A recent study showed that mindfulness meditation may not only be responsible for structural changes in the brain, but also extend our life.

So far, the research has shown some not hugely surprising psychological and cognitive changes: improvements in perception and well-being, for example. However, one result in particular, as documented in the *Observer*, has potentially stunning implications. It appears that meditation might actually help to delay the process of ageing by protecting the caps called telomeres on the ends of our chromosomes.

Why, however, would we want to stay alive if we no longer have a sense of adventure and a curiosity to learn and experience more, moment by moment?

Reducing stress and anger

Anger is a destructive emotion that can trigger the fight-or-flight response in us, even when we are not in physical danger. We may feel the need to express extreme displeasure, which usually takes the form of verbal or sometimes physical attacks, or 'retreating into one's ice-cave' and refusing to communicate at all.

The adrenal and thyroid glands produce adrenaline, noradrenaline and cortisol to fire up our physiology and change our immune response to increase our chances of saving our own life. In a split second, our body changes into a fighting machine that can hit harder, run faster, lift heavy objects, and so on. If, for example, our stressor is a lion that has just escaped from the zoo, we will have the ability to climb up a tree and wait up there until help arrives. As soon as we feel safe again, our parasympathetic nervous system will kick back in. It takes several minutes to get back into parasympathetic calm mode, yet merely a split second to be ready for fight-or-flight.

Everyday stressors

Usually when we have a stressor, however, it is rather different from the occasional lion. For example, it might be a neighbour or a co-worker who triggers the fight-or-flight response in us due to their behaviour, but instead of fighting or fleeing, we stay stewing in our own adrenaline for hours on end.

This can result in immune deficiency, high blood pressure or tension pain in various parts of our body. The other stress chemical, cortisol, particularly affects the brain, which it reaches through our blood circulation. New brain cells – the ones we need for creating new 'neuro-pathways' (new thinking and behaviour patterns) – are destroyed, and the ability to be empathetic diminishes because we are fighting for our own survival, which makes our brain less able to adopt helpful, peaceful solutions. The practices we shall look at now can help us to let go of unresolved interpersonal issues and thus slowly bring us back to a sense of equanimity and peace.

The positive effects of anger

Before we focus on these interventions, I would like to point out that anger can also have a positive effect on our lives (yin and yang) if used as an appropriate force to fire us up when we are fighting injustice, for

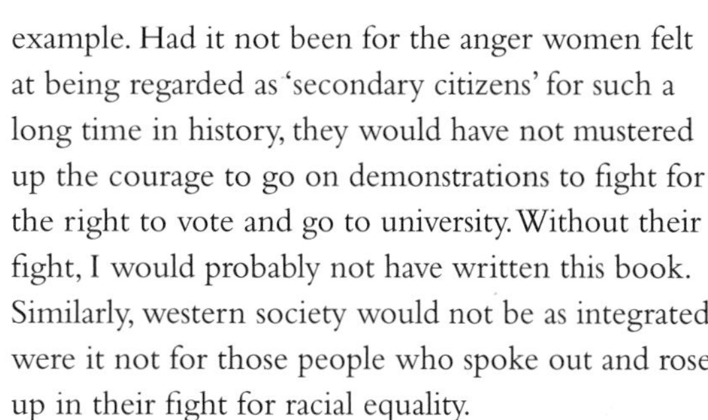

example. Had it not been for the anger women felt at being regarded as 'secondary citizens' for such a long time in history, they would have not mustered up the courage to go on demonstrations to fight for the right to vote and go to university. Without their fight, I would probably not have written this book. Similarly, western society would not be as integrated were it not for those people who spoke out and rose up in their fight for racial equality.

The first exercise that I will share with you is learning how to 'sit with anger', be with it, and see whether by moving towards it, rather than running away from it or feeding aggression, you can find a peaceful resolution for your particular problem.

Practice: Sitting with anger

Find a peaceful area where you will not be interrupted for 10–15 minutes.

1 Sit either in a chair, in a comfortable yet dignified manner, or on the floor with crossed legs, perhaps initially against a wall. Make sure you wrap up in a blanket to stop you getting cold. I always light a candle when I do this exercise, but that is optional. You could also place a gemstone nearby, such as an amethyst for protection, or some flowers as support. If there are others in the house, perhaps put a little note on the door: 'Kindly do not disturb: I am meditating', or use your own way of communicating to others that you need a little peace.

2 Now take your seat and feel your feet firmly on the ground, rooted, your buttocks and lower back supporting you, and your hands resting in your lap. Gently move your awareness to your face and allow all the muscles there to go loose and limp.

3 Focus on your breath by simply noticing it and allowing your body to 'breathe itself'. You need do nothing but sit and taste each breath when it enters your body and observe how it leaves. You may notice that some in-breaths and out-breaths are long and deep while others are short and shallow. After a while, you may even notice that there are little pauses between the in- and out-breaths. Just allow your breathing to take over and simply be the observer. There is no right or wrong way of doing this exercise – just find your personal way of practising.

4 After a while, you may feel a little more settled and ready to experiment with mentally moving towards your anger. You may remember it as a barrage of words or a particular feeling; it may have a colour or shape or form. You may even feel, by allowing thoughts about it to arise, that you are becoming a little more agitated than before, but this is perfectly normal. Now imagine talking to your anger and saying something like: 'I know you are here and I want to understand you. Let me feel you, let me experience you. Give me your all. I am just going to sit here and watch you. I am not going to react and do what I would have done in the past. ' All the while you are focusing on your breathing and 'dancing', as it were, with your anger.

5 Continue doing this for a while and see how you experience 'being with' a discomfort. Finish the exercise when you feel the right moment has arrived.

Practice: Foot scan

In this practice, we are trying to get the furthest away from our 'thinking mind', which is ruminating around 'attack' thoughts, and move into our 'feeling mind'.

1 Start by bringing your awareness to your left foot. Keep the eyes either shut or in soft focus (half-closed); you are not looking at your foot but simply attempting to bring awareness to it. It doesn't matter whether you are sitting or standing. Really feel your foot and slowly guide yourself through the territory of your foot gently and with kindly attention.

You could use words such as:

'I am becoming aware of my left foot, my big toe, my little toe and all the toes in between, even the spaces between the toes, feeling them, sensing them or just knowing that they are there.

'Now I am bringing awareness to the tips of my toes and to my toenails, then to the heel of my foot, the instep and the front part and now the whole sole of my foot.

'I continue bringing attentiveness to my foot as a whole: all the little bones, tendons, blood vessels and, finally, even the skin covering my foot.'

2 Spending a good couple of minutes on your foot in this mindful way will have directed your conscious thinking away from the beliefs that had been feeding your anger initially. This may be enough that you can now further calm the mind by a walking or sound meditation, or by going for a mindful stroll.

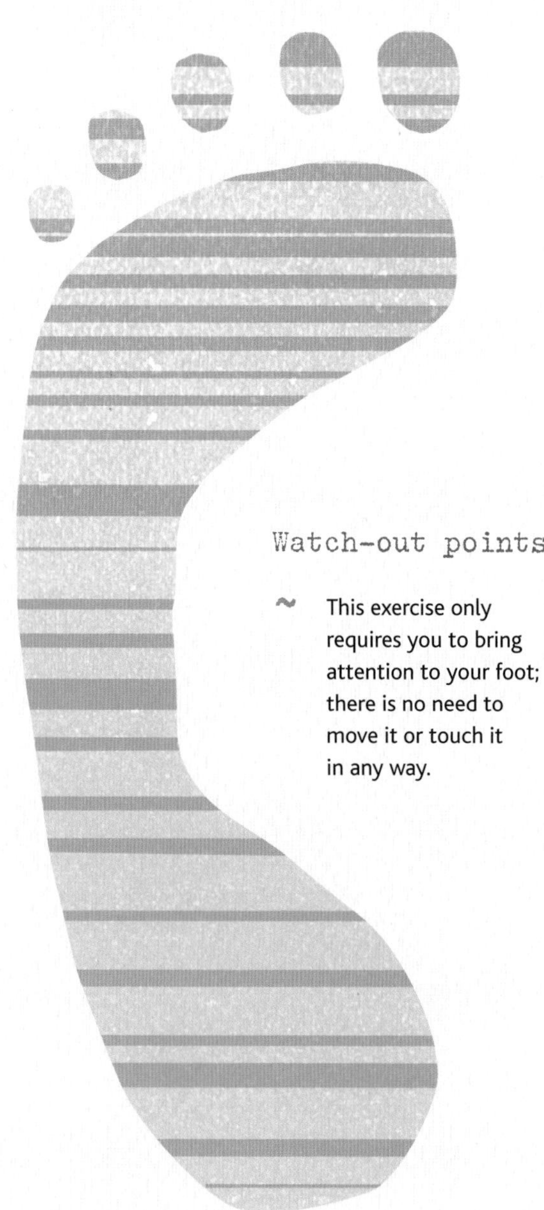

Watch-out points

~ This exercise only requires you to bring attention to your foot; there is no need to move it or touch it in any way.

Case study

Dr N.N. Singh, a very prolific writer and researcher in the field of mindfulness and mental health, developed a mindfulness-based self-discipline plan for a young man with learning difficulties. The client had frequently been very aggressive, breaking and throwing things, which prevented him from staying in community accommodation. He was taught a simple mindfulness intervention. Whenever he felt so angry that he might want to smash or hit something, he was taught to move his attention from the angry thought to a neutral point of his body: the sole of one foot. After rehearsing the footscan several times a week, for a number of weeks, he was able to remain free from reacting aggressively in situations that would in the past have triggered a physical explosion. He was able to keep up this new behaviour for more than six months, which was the minimum timeframe required before he was placed in a community, and then successfully lived in the community without relapsing into his angry behaviour.

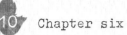

Practice: Cat stretch

Cat stretch can help to release tension in the back, spine, shoulders and neck.

1 Get on your hands and knees on a yoga mat, forming a box position with the frame of your body, placing your wrists directly under the shoulders, and the hips straight under the knees. To protect your knees, you can place a small cushion or folded towel under them. If your wrists feel vulnerable, try rolling up the edge of the mat and placing them on it.

2 Lengthen the entire spine from the top of the head to the tailbone. Inhale, and feel your belly moving away from the spine, then exhale, drawing your navel towards your spine. Repeat this 3 more times, drawing the belly/navel closer to the spine with each exhalation. This creates the abdominal pressure that you need to protect your lower back.

3 Exhale, drawing your navel towards the spine, tucking the tailbone under and, at the same time, moving the chin to the chest. You are now rounding the spine, vertebra by vertebra, into a C-shape, bringing the pubic bone and forehead closer to each other, as if you are dropping yourself over a big beach ball. At the end of the exhalation, in the pause, feel the position.

4 On an inhalation, start reversing the movement. As you slowly and in a controlled way release your belly towards the floor, elongate your spine into the neutral position. Still inhaling, continue the move, lifting the chest and breast bone forwards and up, and look up. Keep the arms strong and the shoulder blades back and down, as if you are pushing them into your back pockets.

5 Repeat the movement 6 times, then return to your starting position. When you have mastered the Cat stretch, having practised it for several days in a row, and feel that your body is ready for a more adventurous pose, try the Sun Salutation practice overleaf. This is a beautiful exercise but you must make sure that you are well before attempting it, and also strong and flexible enough.

Watch-out points

- Draw your navel to your spine throughout the movement in order to protect your lower back.
- Keep the shoulder blades in the mid-back as you round into the C-shape, and let them slide down in the Reverse C-shape.
- Don't bend your arms.
- If you have a lower back problem and/or neck issues, start with a small movement and slowly increase the range of movement.

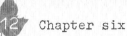

Practice: Simple Sun Salutation

If Sun Salutation is new to you, explore it gently, step by step, over a number of days before you practise it from beginning to end. Pay attention to how you feel and what your body needs at each stage.

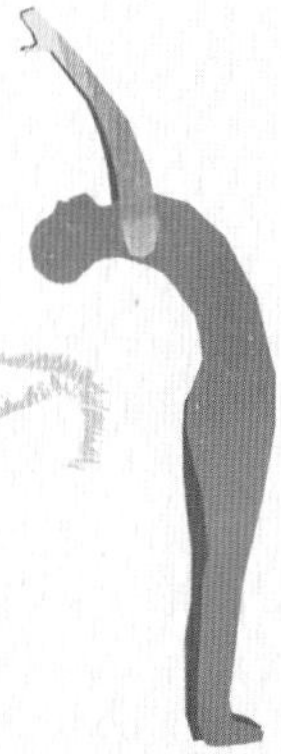

1 Stand in Mountain pose (see page 44), with the hands in Prayer position and the feet hip-width apart.

2 Breathe in gently, lift your arms above your head and follow them with your eyes until you are looking upwards and backwards. You will feel a gentle stretch in your thyroid. Hold until you feel the need to breathe out.

10 Now, very slowly, on an in-breath, roll your spine and head upwards until you are back in Mountain pose.

9 On an out-breath, gently push your leg forwards and place the foot flat on the ground between your hands as shown. Breathe in and let your other leg follow so both legs are between your arms.

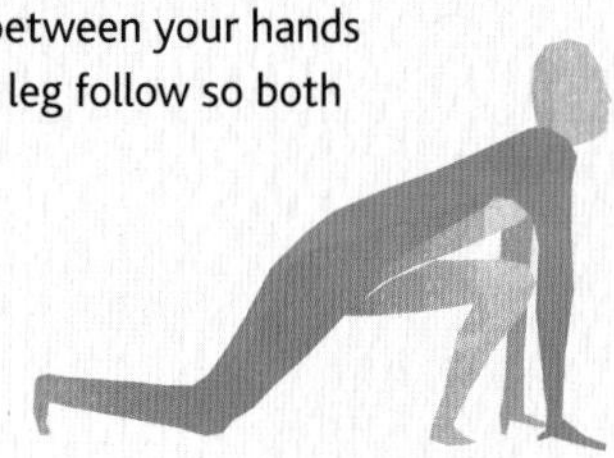

Watch-out points

~ Only engage in physical practices if your body is well and flexible. If not, sit down and visualize the physical practices.

3 On the out-breath, slowly bend forwards, rolling your spine down, vertebra by vertebra, bending your knees as much as you need until your fingertips reach the ground.

4 On the next in-breath, stretch further down, placing your hands with stretched fingers to the left and right of your left knee and moving your right leg and foot backwards. Stretch your leg as far as you can but always remain in your comfort zone.

5 During the same breath, let your left leg follow your right so that both are stretched backwards (Plank position). An easier option is to come down onto your knees, which will serve as a second support to your feet and put less pressure on your wrists.

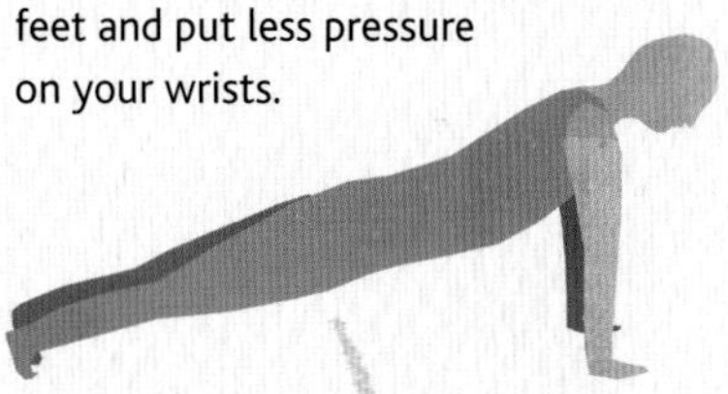

6 On the next out-breath, gently slide down onto the floor, so that you are lying on your belly, forehead down and feet relaxed. Rest for a breath or two.

7 On the next in-breath, place your hands firmly left and right of your breasts and push into the floor, bending and tilting your head and neck upwards and backwards (gentle Cobra pose) as shown. Rest in this posture for a couple of breaths.

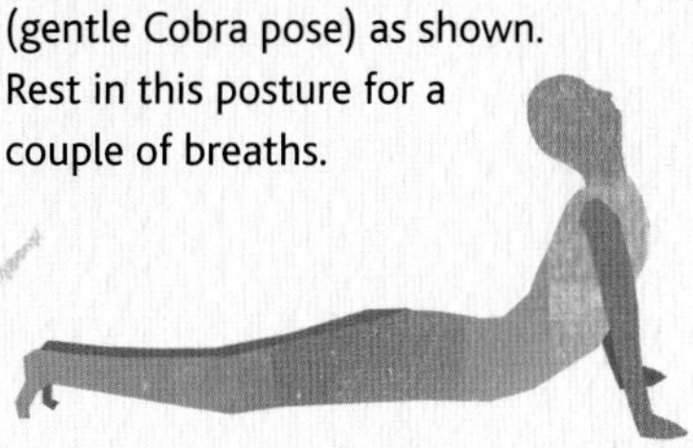

8 On the next out-breath come up into a kneeling box position. Breathe in gently and push upwards. This should not feel uncomfortable, so bent knees are fine. You are now in Downward dog pose. Breathe in and out a couple of times.

To complete a whole round of Sun Salutation, repeat the same routine shown on the previous two pages. Each half-round will combine ten yoga positions smoothly, making 20 for a full round. I really recommend you do this as slowly and mindfully as possible, completing a maximum of five rounds at the beginning. This stretching and cardiovascular practice will release a lot of adrenaline and tension. When you start back in Mountain pose, there is a great possibility that you will be thinking much more calmly and maybe even feeling as strong and peaceful as a mountain. The health benefits of the Sun Salutation are innumerable, such as opening the heart to kindness and knowing, as well as increasing blood oxygenation, which is healing for your heart, brain and other organs. We also experience our elimination channels being activated, helping the body rid itself of toxins. Furthermore, we activate and tone our endocrine system, especially the thyroid, which is the master gland that controls all the other glands. With the increased blood flow to the brain, we feel our mental focus and concentration being more alert. The actual sense of anger and rage may be lessened due to reducing key markers like the stress chemical cortisol, while, simultaneously, the quantity of 'good mood' neurotransmitters like serotonin will increase.

In eastern philosophy, the sun is the 'eye of the world' and an image of, and a pathway to, the divine. When we feel truly ourselves in this moment, and are connected to all other beings, the desire for destruction often seems to vanish.

Practice: Lion pose

The Lion pose helps you to feel powerful and in control. It is a great stretch for the tongue, the throat muscles and many facial muscles. It also releases tension in the chest.

1 Sit on a chair or kneel on the floor with a cushion between your legs.

2 Gently, but actively, draw the navel towards the spine, to help support the lower back. At the same time, lengthen the spine, vertebra by vertebra, towards the ceiling. With the inhalation, allow the chest to expand and, on the following exhalation, roll the shoulders back and down, to support the chest to stay open. Lengthen the crown (the top of your head) towards the ceiling. Rest the palms on your thighs and bend the elbows.

3 Slide the palms towards your knees, gently 'hinging' forwards from your hips, but keeping your arms straight and stopping this movement when the palms cup the knees.

4 Press the palms against your knees and spread your fingers wide. Inhale deeply through the nose. As you exhale, open your mouth wide without bringing tension to the jaw, stretch the tip of your tongue towards the chin as if you wanted to touch it. Raise your eyebrows, roll your eyes back and look to the point between your eyebrows. (Alternatively, look to the tip of your nose.) Exhale through the mouth making the sound 'ha', similar to the roar of a lion. When the exhalation has ended, relax the facial muscles.

5 Repeat step 4 twice more, then return to the start position.

Watch-out points

- Avoid bending your arms when 'roaring'.
- Keep the shoulder blades down in the mid-back.
- Avoid tension in the jaw.

Pebble meditation

Sit down in a comfortable position, either on the floor or on a chair.

Imagine sitting at the edge of a beautiful pond. The sun is shining and you can see some of its rays reflected in the water. There are pond grasses, waterlilies, and blue and green dragonflies circling around. Maybe you hear a frog croaking. Allow yourself to see this pond in all its glory and add any image or sound to the picture that you create in your imagination.

Now see yourself picking up a small, flat pebble and throwing it into the water, watching it sink a little. Notice what thoughts, feelings and sensations you are experiencing right now. Allow the pebble to sink deeper into the water and see whether any sensations, images or feelings change. Finally, allow the pebble to settle at the bottom of the pond. You may even be able to see where it has settled. What do you feel, sense or think now? Are there any messages arising from your consciousness that you need to hear or bring to your awareness?

Remain seated for a little longer and just breathe, from moment to moment… taking care of now.

The Guest House

This being human is a guest house.
Every morning a new arrival.

A joy, a depression, a meanness,
some momentary awareness comes
as an unexpected visitor.

Welcome and entertain them all!
Even if they're a crowd of sorrows,
who violently sweep your house
empty of its furniture,
still, treat each guest honourably.
He may be clearing you out
for some new delight.

The dark thought, the shame, the malice,
meet them at the door laughing,
and invite them in.

Be grateful for whomever comes,
because each has been sent
as a guide from beyond.

JALAL AL-DIN RUMI (1207–1273)

TRANSLATED BY COLEMAN BARKS

Mindful eating

There is hardly a woman in the western hemisphere who has not experienced dissatisfaction with her weight. More and more men are joining the 'club', too. As with other autopilot actions, eating is, for many, no longer a tradition of sitting down and enjoying a meal with others, being grateful for and mindful of the food with which we have been blessed.

We all know, in theory, that our food is a gift, as there are still many places on earth where people are starving, barely surviving on very erratic diets that lack variety as well as nutritional value. However, in the West, the land of plenty, we have not made the best of the great selection available to us. Rather, the opposite is true. Eating frequently becomes something that is quickly fitted in around other activities. Food has also become the bane for many individuals who develop an unhealthy relationship with it, resulting in overeating and obesity, binge eating, or eating as little as possible (anorexia nervosa). This eating disorder is one of the hardest illnesses to treat; it can take up to two years for a client who is committed to following a programme to reconnect to a healthy relationship with food.

A recent study into obese women conducted at the University of California found that those who followed a mindful eating programme (noticing fullness, taste, and so on), combined with a course of meditation to reduce anxiety, saw a marked reduction in their internal visceral fat, which is associated with heart disease, compared to those women who did not follow the programme.

Frequently, we overeat because of stress hormones that float through our system. When we experience the fight-or-flight response, the body thinks it is in danger and prepares for battle, either attacking or quickly getting away and hiding. It then requires readily available resources to fuel all the extra tasks it needs to perform: more blood to the extremities for running or punching harder, improved visual focus, and more blood to certain brain areas. In order to get that extra fuel, we experience an urge to eat sugar or carbohydrates, as they can easily be converted into energy. Are you getting the picture?

At times of great stress, it stands to reason that you will not have an urge to eat carrots or cucumbers, alas! The body cannot differentiate between real danger and perceived danger – even watching a horror film can set off the stress response. The body just does what it evolved to do 700,000 years ago.

Another trigger that lures us into eating more, but not necessarily wholesome – food is loneliness. Eating equals a sense of safety – in the wild, for example, a gazelle will never graze if a lion is on the prowl.

Our lips are the most sensitive skin surface, as you may notice with the Raisin practice on page 122. Children suck dummies or their thumbs to pacify themselves. Adults, on the other hand, eat or drink.

In order to really savour your food, you may want to experiment eating with a smaller fork from a smaller plate. Drinking liquid with a straw, meanwhile, can help you to feel calmer. It is, however, outside the realm of this chapter to go into more details regarding general treatment models for eating disorders. I would simply like to invite all readers to see whether they can actually reintroduce pleasurable, mindful eating into their daily lives. As we all need to eat to survive, we might as well give ourselves time to appreciate our food and also make the practice fun.

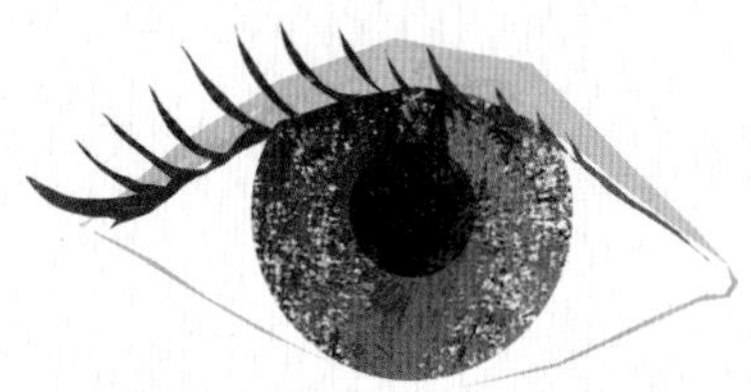

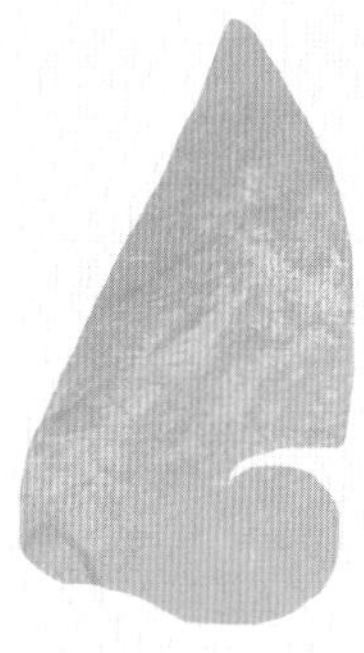

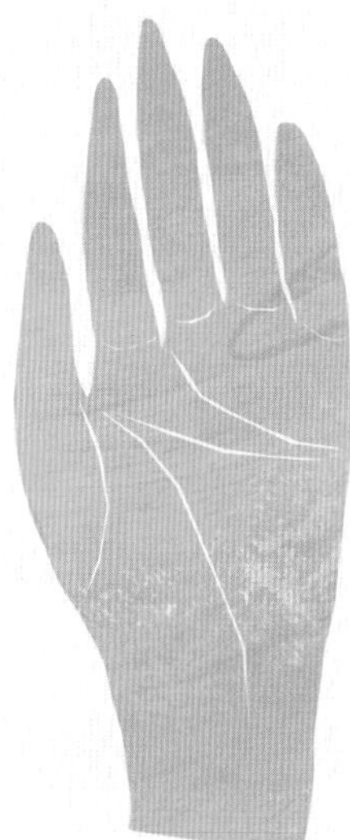

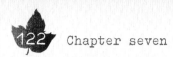

Practice: Raisin practice

This mindful eating practice will help you to reconnect to the pleasure of food. Make sure that you pause after each step.

- Pick up a couple of raisins. Focus on them and imagine you have never seen anything like them before.
- Hold them in the palm of your hand.
- Notice any differences in size, colour, form, weight and shape.
- Look at the raisins even more carefully, observing the ridges and the surface.
- Pick up one of them and explore its texture. Maybe squeeze it or pull it a little.
- Examine the way the light is falling on them.
- Let your sense of vision really have a feast.
- If you start thinking 'Why am I doing this?' or 'This is silly', recognize those thoughts as random thoughts, and return your awareness, without judgement, to viewing these two delightful little things.
- Now smell them, holding one just beneath your nose, and, with each in-breath, notice any aroma that may be there.
- Now place one of them near your ear, squeezing and rubbing it and checking whether a sound is apparent. Is there? Let yourself be surprised.
- Now look again at the object and then gently touch the surface of your lips with one of them. Does that skin contact feel any different from the one you were experiencing when holding the raisin between the thumb and finger?
- Now, slowly take the object towards your mouth, feeling your arm rising effortlessly to the right position, perhaps also feeling your mouth watering.

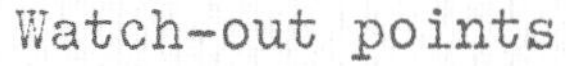

Watch-out points

- You might use chocolate, nuts or any quick snack food as an alternative, and adapt the practice accordingly.
- Be mindful of not rushing when you swallow to avoid choking.

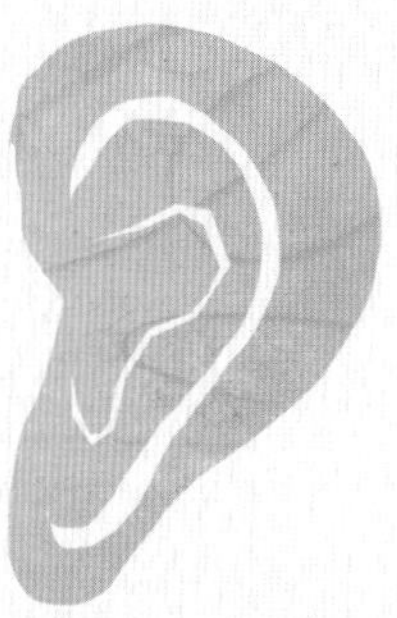

- Gently place the object in your mouth without biting it. Notice how it is 'received', exploring the sensations of having it in your mouth.
- When you are ready, very consciously take a bite into it and notice the flavours that are released.
- Slowly chew it, noticing the saliva in your mouth and the change in consistency of the raisin. Observe anything that may be completely new to you.
- Then, when you feel ready, swallow the pulpy mass, seeing if you can first detect the intention to swallow as it comes up, so that even this is experienced consciously before you actually swallow it.
- Finally, see if you can follow the sensations of swallowing, sensing the raisin moving down to your stomach, and also realizing that your body is now exactly one raisin fuller. What are you still tasting in your mouth? What is your tongue doing now? Is there a desire to eat the second raisin?
- After this everyday practice, you may feel somewhat calmer and more settled. Just imagine if you ate each spoonful of a meal – not every meal but maybe one a day – in the same manner. Alternatively, you could try eating an apple or drinking your favourite drink in this way.
- Engage in this practice with childlike curiosity and playfulness.

Drinking tea

The twentieth-century Viennese writer Peter Altenberg tells the following story about the joy and deep satisfaction of drinking tea:

Six o'clock in the evening is approaching. I can sense it drawing near. Not quite as intensely as children feel Christmas Eve, but creeping up all the same. At six o'clock on the dot I drink tea, a celebratory enjoyment devoid of disappointment in this ailing existence. Something that makes you realize that you have the power of calming happiness in your hands. Even the action of pouring fresh water into my beautiful, wide half-litre nickel kettle gives me pleasure. I wait patiently for it to boil, listening out for the whistling sound, the singing of the water.

I have a huge, deep, round mug made of red-brick-coloured Wedgwood. The tea from Café Central smells like meadows in the countryside.

The tea has a golden yellow hue, like fresh hay. It never gets too brown, but remains light and delicate. I drink it mindfully and very slowly. The tea has a stimulating effect on my nervous system. Everything in life seems to be more bearable and lighter thereafter.

Drinking my tea at six o'clock never seems to lose its power over me. Every day I long for it as intensively as the day before, and when I drink it I lovingly embrace it into my being.

(Translated and adapted by Patrizia Collard from *Sonnenuntergang im Prater* by Peter Altenberg)

Revisiting the body scan meditation: Nourishing the body

In an earlier part of the book (see pages 74–7), we practised the body scan lying down with our legs falling open. This time we choose a posture that is more alert. So we either sit on a chair or lie down with the legs in a triangle position. We journey through the body once more, focusing mainly on the torso in order to really get in touch with those areas of the body that help us feel connected to the process of nourishment.

1 Wearing loose clothing, find a comfortable position and make sure you will not get cold (maybe use a blanket or a shawl).

2 Start with your head and bring awareness to the crown of your head, the back and the forehead. Bring awareness to your entire face: all your features one by one. Move further down and bring awareness to your neck and shoulders, arms and hands, buttocks, legs and feet. Make sure that your feet are firmly grounded on the surface they are standing on. If you are lying down, feel the soles of your feet pressing against each other.

3 Now bring alertness to your torso: the back, the spine, the chest and then the abdomen. Notice how the breath moves in and out of your body, with particular focus on those areas that rise and fall with the breath.

4 Now bring awareness to your digestive organs: the stomach and the colon. Rest with awareness in this part of your body. Gently remember that in these areas all nourishment is received and digested. The energy that is created through this process is now fuelling your whole body. Smile into these areas of your body, bringing kindly awareness and gratitude to them and, on each in-breath, allow oxygen to flow into them and releasing any tension, discomfort or critical thoughts on the out-breath.

5 Stay for a while with the breath in this part of your body until you feel a sense of calm and kindly appreciation.

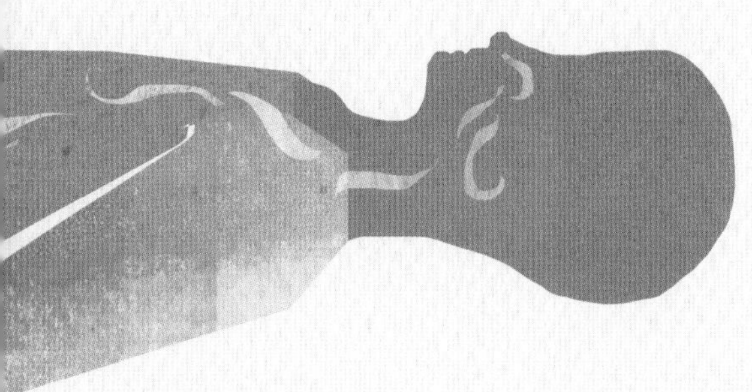

Watch-out points

~ Prop your head up with a pillow and try not to fall asleep. The intention of the body scan is to stay awake to the experience of being alive.

Gratitude

In addition to mindful eating and drinking, we can also open up to a sense of gratitude for the wonderful variety of food and drinks we are able to buy or grow. We may think with humility how each item we consume started, perhaps as a little seed that was planted and tended by someone, and then harvested, transported and maybe prepared into some new 'creation'. Thereafter it was delivered to a shop where you chose and paid for it at the till. Just think of this long chain of events and the numerous people involved in getting your food to you.

Gratitude and appreciation help us turn towards joy and gladness. These emotions, in turn, create chemicals of well-being and peace in our whole body. There are studies that show that the regular practice of gratitude and appreciation (for example, writing down the experiences you feel grateful for in a notebook) can lead to better physical health, less stress and a more optimistic outlook on life.

Practice: Gratitude meditation

Find a peaceful spot where you can sit down and write in your notebook and meditate.

~ Give yourself a few minutes and note down all things you are grateful for in your life (such as friendships, things about yourself, your body, your home, pleasurable memorie, and so on.)

~ Read through your list and internally give words of thanks to each point you noted down. For example: Thanks for my beautiful smile, thanks for my special favourite mug, thanks for my last holiday.... When you give thanks, really tune into all five senses as best as you can.

~ Bring awareness to this moment. What are you grateful for right here and now. How does this feel in your body and where do you feel it? Gently breathe and sit with gratitude for a little while longer.

Sea Miracle

Like a planet
Deep blue-green liquid
Beckons us
Modern mermaids
Enter deep waters
Breathing bubble sound
All life starts here
Two tiny squids
Frilly edges fluttering
She feeds him lovingly
A nourishing embrace
More lovers
Walking Pegasus fish
Miniature dragons
Roaming the sandy bottom
Forever together
Blending into the speckled reef
Life beyond beauty
Serenity.

PATRIZIA COLLARD

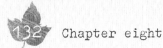

Self-acceptance: loving kindness and compassion

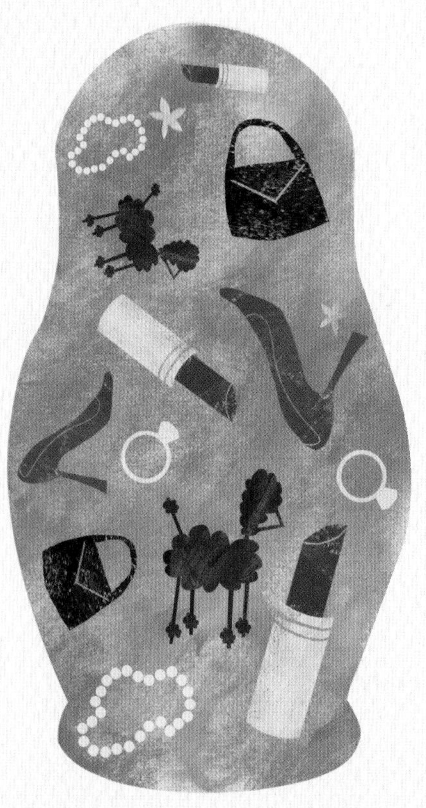

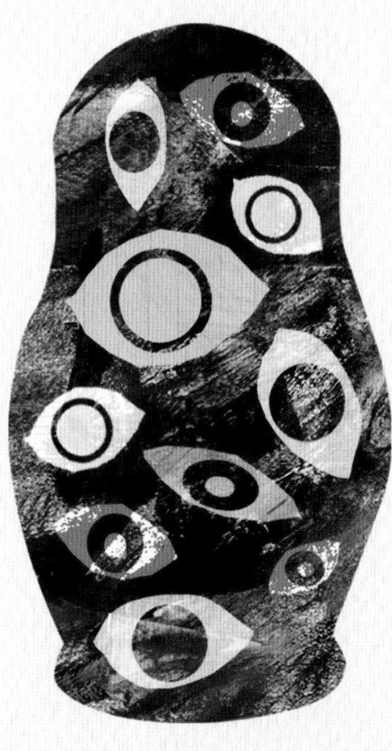

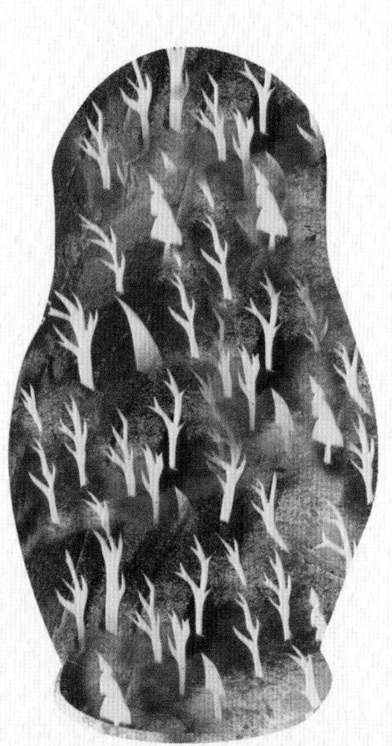

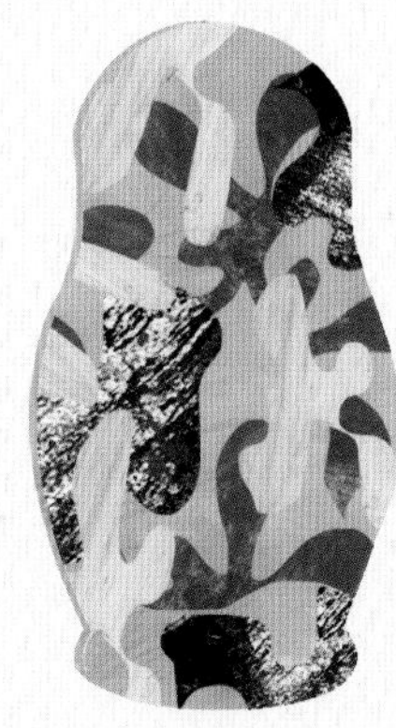

In the western hemisphere, it is rare that people are really happy, content with who and what they are and how their lives are unfolding. Children, however, are often blissfully unaware that there may be something wrong with them in the eyes of some adults, but actually they feel, up to a certain age, okay with who they are.

It is our system of evaluating everything, and having to be better than everybody else, that has created the 'ego states' that on the one hand are very demanding and on the other very self-centred and destructive. There seems to be an ongoing struggle to improve oneself, to beat oneself up and to feel dissatisfied. When I talk about self-acceptance, I actually do mean 'warts or wrinkles and all'. The aim is to get to the point of saying, 'This is who I am and this is okay.'

Making sense of self-acceptance

The human condition is one of imperfection. We are all the same. I attended a conference in 2005 in Gothenburg, entitled 'Making Sense of the 21st Century'. Aaron Beck, a famous psychotherapist, and the Dalai Lama were in conversation. The former asked the latter what Buddhists did in order to help people feel worthy of love and self-acceptance. The Dalai Lama found it very difficult to make sense of the question, and for several minutes he discussed it with his translator, to make sure he really understood what he was being asked. His answer took a good ten minutes to arise in his awareness before he could share it with the audience. In his culture, each living thing is worthy of life and love. The question of acceptance does not exist. It is a given that you are accepted simply because you are part of creation.

Self-compassion

The Buddha supposedly said in a famous teaching that we could search the whole world over and not find anyone more deserving of love than ourselves. Yet, as we have sometimes discovered, it is often harder to feel the same kindness towards ourselves as we would towards someone else.

Self-compassion can be seen as the yin to mindfulness – the yang. We need to be kind and accepting of ourselves when we don't manage to be mindful, and in the same vein, we need mindfulness to observe our own defeating self-critical behaviour and thoughts. If we can learn to truly accept ourselves with compassion, it may be much easier to be 'here and now', and not be drawn back to old fears, guilt or worries, or towards future goals that we feel we need in order to achieve.

Studies have shown that self-compassion can have a number of health benefits, such as being less self-critical, which in turn reduces criticism of others. It also lowers stress chemicals such as cortisol, and hence improves our immune system and cognitive functioning. Lastly, it increases self-soothing and self-encouragement, which tend to make us stronger, more adventurous and more resilient.

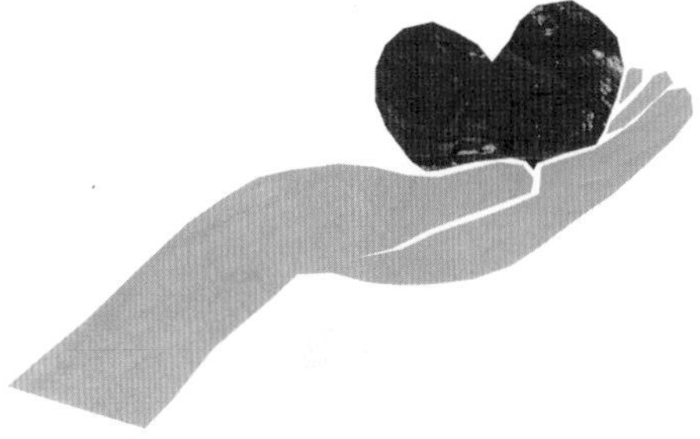

Practice: The big 'I'

Take a large sheet of paper and draw on it a big letter 'I'. The big 'I' represents you as a whole, all the actions you've ever done, all aspects of your body, mind and talents etc. Then, over the period of a week, write down, within the big 'I', little 'i's, whenever they happen to come to your awareness – choose one coloured pen for all the things and actions you like about yourself, and another colour for the things and actions you feel need improving. Each little 'i' should represent one aspect only. For example, I would write in green: 'enjoys meeting people', 'loves singing', 'good at cooking', 'nice eyes'. Then I would put in red: 'increase patience', 'improve office organization', 'allow for more play time'. A big 'I' could contain hundreds of little 'i's, but we often reject ourselves because of just a couple of little 'i's which need improvement or simply acceptance – noone will have all positive or all negative traits. We are all yin and yang.

All these little 'i's should be scattered in no particular order. You can even ask others who know you well to add some of the little 'i's about you. It is a wonderful practice to really see, in large scale, how we all consist of a broad choice of behaviour traits and personal characteristics. Nobody will be either a complete failure or perfect. This is the human condition and to accept it fully is the starting point for change.

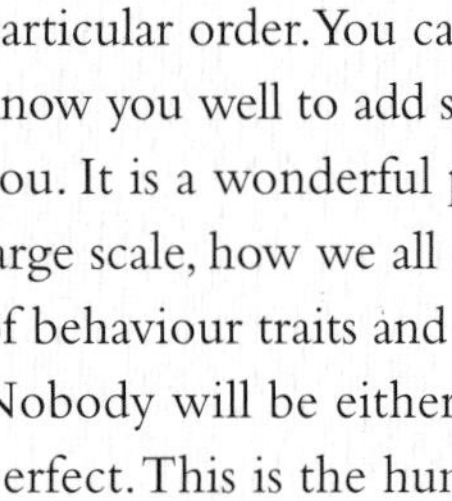

Case study

A mindfulness teacher, who is also a psychiatrist, wanted to see how extreme anxiety would actually affect the brain. One of his close friends suffered from a phobia of birds, and she offered to participate in this experiment for the sake of scientific advance.

It was agreed that she would be told a story about birds while being observed in the FMRI scanner. Her brain response was being scanned while the psychiatrist evoked her phobia. He told her how initially one and then more and more pigeons would fly towards her and sit near her or even on her head or shoulder. Within less than a minute, the participant was obviously having a panic attack. Her breathing became faster and shallower, and her brain showed a significant increase of activation in those parts that deal with threat and set off the stress response – the amygdala and hypothalamus. Suddenly, however, the anxiety started to reduce, and the scanner showed that the brain was slowly returning to a calm state. When the participant was asked what she had done to stop the panic attack, she said: 'When I got more and more frightened and could stand it no longer, I started praying. I visualized the Virgin Mary standing next to me, smiling and putting her hand on my shoulder. The birds... I am not sure whether they disappeared, but I was no longer concerned about them. I felt so protected and loved.'

Practice: Metta meditation

Metta is usually translated as 'loving kindness', and this form of meditation is very popular in Buddhism. By practising it, you may find you are able to deal with situations with greater ease and lightness. I truly feel that it is a very empowering tool for transformation.

It can be helpful to visualize, in the centre of your chest, your 'emotional' heart, an image of yourself as you are now or as you were as a little child, perhaps supported by a loving elder. If visualizing is difficult for you, then try just seeing your name written in the centre of your heart.

The Metta practice starts with the pure intention that we wish to increase self-compassion from within. We may use the analogy of planting a seed, which we tend through the practice until it grows into a beautiful flower or a tree.

'May I be safe and protected.'
'May I be peaceful.'
'May I live at ease and with kindness.'

Week by week we expand the practice. In week two, after meditating on ourselves, we add somebody we love and care for:

'May you be safe and protected.'
'May you be peaceful.'
'May you live at ease and with kindness.'

We finally expand the practice still further to include people we hardly know, people who may have caused us irritation or hurt:

'May all beings be safe and protected.'
'May all beings be peaceful.'
'May all beings live at ease and with kindness.'

With this practice, we start with the mere intention of loving kindness, but experience has shown me that persisting with it can wonderfully enrich our lives. If every one of us just managed to touch one 'other' through this practice, the world would indeed be a safer, kinder and more peaceful place in which to live.

Plant so that your
own heart will grow

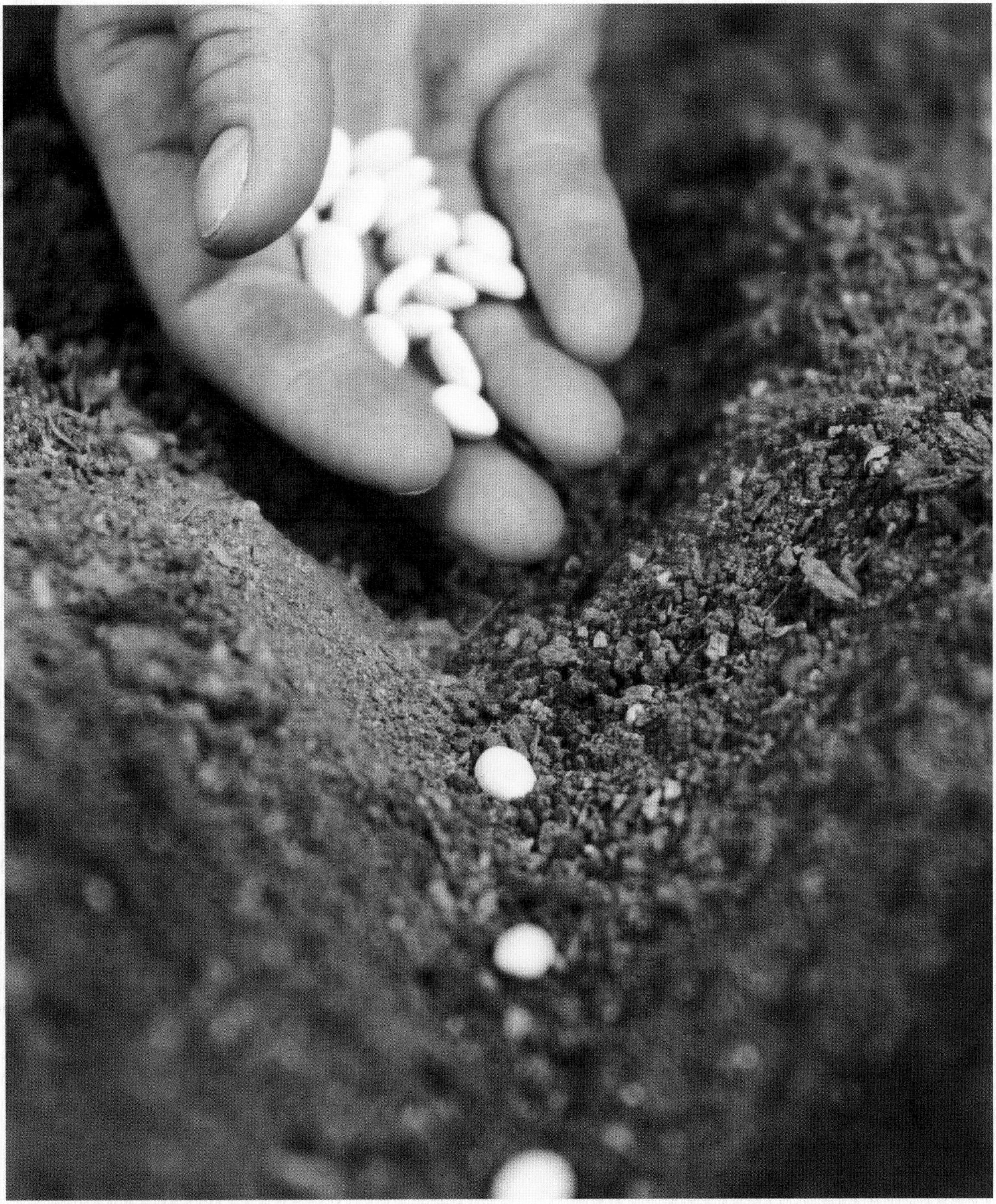

Gift

Give Love a chance
Give Life a chance
he says
eyes glowing
soft husky words
gently smiling
stroking my mind
a chance
you want
one chance
I give you
one for
thee
one for me
one for Love
one for Life
one for him
who made us
met us
linked us too
five chances in all
is this enough
five times five
then
more
five times five times
five
and should this not suffice
I give you my all
all that I have
I give you Me

PATRIZIA COLLARD

Practice: Smile into the body – a brief sitting practice

1 Find a comfortable, quiet and dignified sitting posture. Join the hands with both thumbs and the fingers of one hand resting in those of the other.

2 Start this practice by focusing on your breathing. Let each breath unfold by itself, neither lengthening it, nor expanding and deepening it. Allow the body to breathe itself, and pay witness to this miraculous breath, coming and going.

3 When you feel settled, having breathed like this for a few minutes, allow a gentle smile to arise on your face. Notice how it softens all the facial muscles and how, breath by breath, this softening and relaxing moves further and further into every cell of your body. Soon your whole body will be a gentle, soft smile.

4 Sit with this for a while and simply 'be', moment by moment.

Watch-out points

~ Allow any thoughts – whether bad or good – to pass you by like a cloud in the sky.

A Daily Meditation

Let us be still for a few moments,
without moving even our little finger
so that a hush descends upon us.
There would be no place to go,
nor to come from,
for we would have arrived in this extraordinary moment;
there would be a stillness and silence,
that would fill all of our senses,
where all things would find their rest.
Everything would then be together in a deep connection,
putting an end to 'us and them', this against that;
we would not move in these brief moments,
for that would disturb this palpable presence;
there would be nothing to be said nor done,
for life would embrace us in this wondrous meeting,
and take us into its arms as a loving friend.

CHRISTOPHER TITMUS

Journey's end

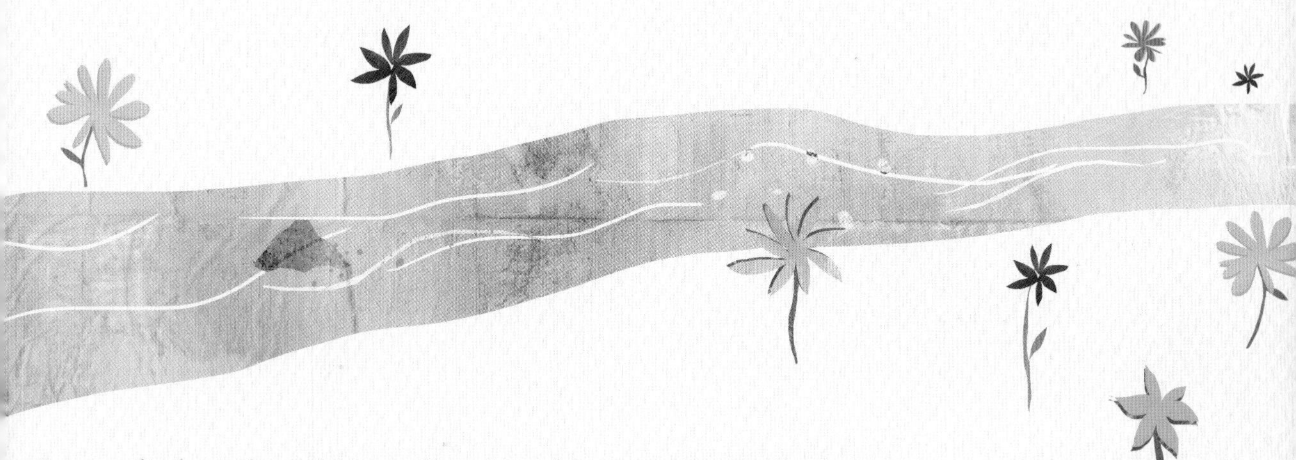

I am a little sad, and I am allowing this emotion to be here, just for now. Our journey into mindfulness is coming to an end. Yet I know it really is only the beginning of another chapter, another adventure, and I hope this book will help you to be inspired to live your life moment by moment, knowing that the only thing we can be certain of is that everything changes all the time.

The beautiful gift that mindfulness gives me is to fully accept everything and anything that life offers me. This insight has freed me – and keeps freeing me – from the old mind-patterns of fear and expectation. 'It is what it is' and is okay. I am still learning, but day by day I am more certain that any one of us is like a beautiful diamond that only needs a little bit of cutting here and there before it sparkles all over.

An uncut diamond tends to look just like any stone, yet beneath that surface lies miraculous clarity and beauty.

Mindfulness is an attitude rather than a skill. Whenever we feel we have reconnected to the old treadmill of autopilot, we may choose, if we so wish, to step out and start again.

Using mindfulness every day

A client who attended one of my courses told me right at the end that 'everyday mindfulness' had changed her life. The practices of mindful movement and meditation had been useful too, but what really turned her life around was changing her attitude to something she had to do every day, and had despised until recently.

Prior to attending the course she had read research papers that indicated that practising mindfulness had very beneficial effects on skin disorders. She suffered from severe eczema, which she could only control by means of a rigid regime of applying cream to her entire body first thing in the morning and last thing at night.

She was initially a little disappointed not to be miraculously healed of her disease, but then she accepted that this was still an option, which might happen one day soon or slowly over time, if at all.

However, one thing she could already do now was to apply the cream mindfully to each part of her body, not rushing it, breathing gently into every part she was attending to, and also bringing a sense of gratitude for the fact that this regime actually kept the disease under control. It became a kindly ritual with a very different energy, rather than the hugely disliked ordeal it had been before.

How can we turn a particular moment into a special experience, if we only count those moments that are 'perfect'? We would miss out a lot of learning and experiencing. It would also create another problem: so-called 'perfect' moments are often so wonderful that we do not want them to pass. So we cling to them, which ultimately destroys all joy, just as love is destroyed if we put it in a golden cage. Allowing ourselves and others to have free will, and accepting life as being an ever changing experience where each moment is unique – this final analysis is the idea of mindful awareness.

On a larger scale, mindfulness leads us sooner or later to the insight that we are all interconnected, that none of us is ever truly alone and that each of us, in one way or another, needs the other.

I am not trying to persuade you simply to believe me, but to invite you to think it through. Even if you were to live alone and grow your own food and build your own home, where would you get all the necessary tools and ingredients? Nature, living beings and the universe are all a part of each other.

Mindful living eventually leads to more awareness and a compassion towards all that is, was and will be.

So the dance of life has purpose – however long we engage in it. In *Happy For No Reason*, research by self-help author Marci Shimoff shows that that without purpose, human beings become very unhappy, even if all their physical needs are met and satisfied.

Whatever your life path is, mindfulness can enrich every action each day, as long as it does not become a 'must' but remains a 'want' and a glorious experiment.

Mindful

My awareness settled comfortably
In the seat of the present moment
Open to the symphony of life

ANNA (A FRIEND)

A mindful day

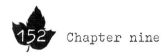

On waking, you may focus for a little while on your breathing, just observing it with gentle curiosity. You may want to smile into your body before getting up, breathing gently into every part. Continue having a mindful bath or shower, brushing your teeth with awareness and mindfully getting ready for the day.

Some people like to meditate in the morning, others in the evening or even at different times of the day. However, it is a good idea to pencil this special 'meeting with yourself' into your diary.

Sounds can be a lovely way to connect mindfully with life: the patter of raindrops or the soft sighing of the wind, but also the whistling of a kettle, the enormous variety of birdsong or the laughter of happy strangers passing by.

You may decide to do the Breathing practices (see pages 62–7) a few times a day, maybe every time you wash your hands or enjoy a drink.

Each meal of the day can be a call to mindfulness and gratitude. If possible, and without a sense of duty, recall how many steps were necessary to create this lovely soup in the bowl in front of you. Freely connect to the gardeners who planted and harvested the vegetables, the potter who created the bowl, the cook who prepared the meal. Really taste the dish and see whether you can guess how many ingredients went into it. The simplest meal can become a feast with a little 'dash' of awareness.

Communicating with others is another wholesome part of the practice. Listen to yourself answering the phone or having a conversation. Are you mindful of how you speak and listen, giving space to the other person and choosing words with honesty but without the need to win or score points?

When there are moments that might in the past have amounted to nothing or to frustration, such as being stuck in traffic, you could try to breathe mindfully, or listen to music – really listen – or simply take in your surroundings – really seeing life as it presents itself at that given moment.

When the day is coming to an end, you may want to note down in a diary your 'EGS' of the day: what did you *Enjoy* today, what are you *Grateful* for and what are you *Satisfied* with – this could be something as mundane as having made a particular phone call or paid a bill; just a little action is enough. Before switching off the light, you are once again invited to connect to your body with kindly awareness, smiling and breathing into it.

A Gaelic Blessing

Deep peace of the running wave to you
Deep peace of the flowing air to you
Deep peace of the quiet earth to you
Deep peace of the shining stars to you
Deep peace of the gentle night to you
Moon and stars pour their healing light on you
Deep peace to you
Deep peace to you

ANONYMOUS

Index

Author's acknowledgements

I want to thank all the fantastic people who helped to shape *Journey into Mindfulness* and either contributed factual aspects or wise inspiration, especially:

Helen Stephenson who has suggested and contributed so much to the physical exercises in this volume. When I first participated in her Yoga/Pilates retreats I fell in love with her way of teaching and being, and I feel honoured that she shared so much with me.

Bernhard, for being my Love, Inspiration and Nourishment for my soul.

Dan, my wonderful and insightful son, for his critical appraisal of many aspects of this book and whose suggestions made the reading of it even smoother and more joyful.

Toby, my young one, whose smiles and hugs gave ongoing sustenance to me.

My students Suzanne, Ann-Marie and Anna who contributed their wonderful poems and lyrics to this adventure.

Christopher Titmus for allowing me to use his Daily Meditation. Thank you.

Liz Dean, my publisher who found me, inspired me, allowed me to write freely and reined me in when I got over-excited. She walked with me through the entire writing process and supported me so wonderfully.

Sybella Stephens, senior editor, whose kindness and giving feedback helped tremendously in the later stages of writing.

Tybalt, our young cat for being truly in the moment.

All other creatures 'big and small' who knowingly or unknowingly offered inspiration and kindness.

Photographic credits

Alamy Ann and Steve Toon 71; Corbis Flirt 142; Cultura Creative 2 below left; D Hurst 2 below right; Design Pics Inc 2 centre right; Fancy 35; KC Photography 24 above; Moodboard 120; PhotoAlto 14, 78, 82; es-cuisine 68; PhotosIndia.com 26; Piotr Skubisz 37
Corbis Clark Dunbar 18; Eye Ubiquitous/ www.flowerphotos.com/Michael Peuckert 150; Image Plan 45; Minden Pictures/Ingo Arndt 72, Scott Leslie 130; Onoky/Eric Audras 2 above right; Paul Edmondson 146; Peter Johnson 24 below; PhotoAlto/Michele Constantini 60; RelaXimages 152; Richard Hamilton Smith 138; Simon Plant 20; Topic Photo Agency 24 centre
Getty Images AFP/Hoang Dinh Ham 13; Andrew Bret Wallis 42; Blue Line Pictures 38; Brian Gordon Green 116; Chua Kong Ping 86; Datacraft Co Ltd 10; Fredrik Skold 128; Garden Picture Library/Mark Bolton 2 above centre; Godong/Robert Harding World Imagery 74; Guido Mieth 17; Jessie Jean 49; JGI/Tom Grill 52; Kathy Collins 134-5; Kenneth Barker 154; Kristian Sekulic 2 above left; Liz Spindler Photography Inc 32; Mark Scott 62; Martin Ruegner 100; Michael Hitoshi 144; RK Studio 89; Ryan McVay 98; T-Pool/Stock4B 157; Tom Haseltine 40-1; Torsten Karock 28-9; Yamini Chao 124
Glow Images Glow Botanica 46
Michael Wilson 106
SuperStock Joe Fox/age footstock 136
Thinkstock iStockphoto 85, 141; Janey Airey 56; Ron Chapple Studios 30